חַיִּים חֵן וָחֶסֶד בְּבְשָׂרֵנוּ וְעַל ... שֶׁ... שֶׁלְּ... שֶׁ... דָּ...

בְכָ... נְתַתָּנוּ וְעַל אֲכִילַת מָזוֹן שָׁאַתָּה זָן וּמְפַרְנֵס אוֹתָנוּ תָּמִיד

... וְעַל צִיּוֹן מִשְׁכַּן רַחֵם־נָא יְיָ אֱלֹהֵינוּ עַל יִשְׂרָאֵל עַמֶּךָ וְעַל יְרוּשָׁלַיִם עִיר

הַקָּדוֹשׁ שֶׁנִּקְרָא שְׁמְךָ כְּבוֹדֶךָ וְעַל מַלְכוּת בֵּית דָּוִד מְשִׁיחֶךָ. וְעַל הַבַּיִת הַגָּדוֹל וְה...

הַרְוַח לָנוּ יְיָ אֱלֹהֵינוּ עָלָיו. אֱלֹהֵינוּ אָבִינוּ רְעֵנוּ זוּנֵנוּ פַּרְנְסֵנוּ וְכַלְכְּלֵנוּ וְהַרְוִיחֵנוּ וְ...

מַתְּנַת בָּשָׂר וָדָם וְלֹא מְהֵרָה מִכָּל־צָרוֹתֵינוּ וְנָא אַל־תַּצְרִיכֵנוּ יְיָ אֱלֹהֵינוּ לֹא לִידֵי...

הָרְחָבָה שֶׁלֹּא נֵבוֹשׁ לִידֵי הַלְוָאתָם. כִּי אִם לְיָדְךָ הַמְּלֵאָה הַפְּתוּחָה הַקְּדוֹשָׁה וְ...

... עִי. הַשַּׁבָּת הַגָּדוֹל הַזֶּה רְצֵה וְהַחֲלִיצֵנוּ יְיָ אֱלֹהֵינוּ בְּמִצְוֹתֶיךָ וּבְמִצְוַת יוֹם הַשְּׁבִי...

... וְלָנוּחַ בּוֹ בְּאַהֲבָה וְהַקָּדוֹשׁ הַזֶּה. כִּי יוֹם זֶה גָּדוֹל וְקָדוֹשׁ הוּא לְפָנֶיךָ לִשְׁבָּת בּוֹ...

... ה וְיָגוֹן וַאֲנָחָה בְּיוֹם כְּמִצְוַת רְצוֹנֶךָ: וּבִרְצוֹנְךָ הָנִיחַ לָנוּ יְיָ אֱלֹהֵינוּ שֶׁלֹּא תְהֵא צָרָ...

... יִם עִיר קָדְשֶׁךָ. כִּי מְנוּחָתֵנוּ. וְהַרְאֵנוּ יְיָ אֱלֹהֵינוּ בְּנֶחָמַת צִיּוֹן עִירֶךָ וּבְבִנְיַן יְרוּשָׁלַ...

יִשְׁמַע וְיִפָּקֵד וְיִזָּכֵר אֱלֹהֵינוּ וֵאלֹהֵי אֲבוֹתֵינוּ, יַעֲלֶה וְיָבֹא, וְיַגִּיעַ, וְיֵרָאֶה, וְיֵרָצֶה וְ...

ךְ: וְזִכְרוֹן יְרוּשָׁלַיִם זִכְרוֹנֵנוּ וּפִקְדוֹנֵנוּ וְזִכְרוֹן אֲבוֹתֵינוּ. וְזִכְרוֹן מָשִׁיחַ בֶּן דָּוִד עַבְדֶ...

לְטוֹבָה לְחֵן וּלְחֶסֶד עִיר קָדְשֶׁךָ. וְזִכְרוֹן כָּל עַמְּךָ בֵּית יִשְׂרָאֵל לְפָנֶיךָ. לִפְלֵטָה...

אֱלֹהֵינוּ בּוֹ לְטוֹבָה וּלְרַחֲמִים לְחַיִּים וּלְשָׁלוֹם בְּיוֹם חַג הַמַּצּוֹת הַזֶּה. זָכְרֵנוּ יְיָ...

שׁוּעָה וְרַחֲמִים חוּס וּפָקְדֵנוּ בוֹ לִבְרָכָה. וְהוֹשִׁיעֵנוּ בוֹ לְחַיִּים טוֹבִים. וּבִדְבַר יְ...

עַל בְּרִיתְךָ שֶׁחָתַמְתָּ שֶׁהוֹצֵאתָנוּ יְיָ אֱלֹהֵינוּ מֵאֶרֶץ מִצְרַיִם וּפְדִיתָנוּ מִבֵּית עֲבָדִים וְ...

צַל חַיִּים חֵן וָחֶסֶד בִּבְשָׂרֵנוּ וְעַל תּוֹרָתְךָ שֶׁלִּמַּדְתָּנוּ וְעַל חֻקֶּיךָ שֶׁהוֹדַעְתָּנוּ וְ...

בְּכָל יוֹם וּבְכָל עֵת שֶׁחוֹנַנְתָּנוּ וְעַל אֲכִילַת מָזוֹן שָׁאַתָּה זָן וּמְפַרְנֵס אוֹתָנוּ תָּמִיד

... וְעַל צִיּוֹן מִשְׁכַּן רַחֵם־נָא יְיָ אֱלֹהֵינוּ עַל יִשְׂרָאֵל עַמֶּךָ וְעַל יְרוּשָׁלַיִם עִיר...

הַקָּדוֹשׁ שֶׁנִּקְרָא שְׁמְךָ כְּבוֹדֶךָ וְעַל מַלְכוּת בֵּית דָּוִד מְשִׁיחֶךָ. וְעַל הַבַּיִת הַגָּדוֹל וְה...

הַרְוַח לָנוּ יְיָ אֱלֹהֵינוּ עָלָיו. אֱלֹהֵינוּ אָבִינוּ רְעֵנוּ זוּנֵנוּ פַּרְנְסֵנוּ וְכַלְכְּלֵנוּ וְהַרְוִיחֵנוּ וְ...

מַתְּנַת בָּשָׂר וָדָם וְלֹא מְהֵרָה מִכָּל־צָרוֹתֵינוּ וְנָא אַל־תַּצְרִיכֵנוּ יְיָ אֱלֹהֵינוּ לֹא לִידֵי...

הָרְחָבָה שֶׁלֹּא נֵבוֹשׁ לִידֵי הַלְוָאתָם. כִּי אִם לְיָדְךָ הַמְּלֵאָה הַפְּתוּחָה הַקְּדוֹשָׁה וְ...

... עִי. הַשַּׁבָּת הַגָּדוֹל הַזֶּה רְצֵה וְהַחֲלִיצֵנוּ יְיָ אֱלֹהֵינוּ בְּמִצְוֹתֶיךָ וּבְמִצְוַת יוֹם הַשְּׁבִי...

... וְלָנוּחַ בּוֹ בְּאַהֲבָה וְהַקָּדוֹשׁ הַזֶּה. כִּי יוֹם זֶה גָּדוֹל וְקָדוֹשׁ הוּא לְפָנֶיךָ לִשְׁבָּת בּוֹ...

... ה וְיָגוֹן וַאֲנָחָה בְּיוֹם כְּמִצְוַת רְצוֹנֶךָ: וּבִרְצוֹנְךָ הָנִיחַ לָנוּ יְיָ אֱלֹהֵינוּ שֶׁלֹּא תְהֵא צָרָ...

... יִם עִיר קָדְשֶׁךָ. כִּי מְנוּחָתֵנוּ. וְהַרְאֵנוּ יְיָ אֱלֹהֵינוּ בְּנֶחָמַת צִיּוֹן עִירֶךָ וּבְבִנְיַן יְרוּשָׁלַ...

יִשְׁמַע וְיִפָּקֵד וְיִזָּכֵר אֱלֹהֵינוּ וֵאלֹהֵי אֲבוֹתֵינוּ, יַעֲלֶה וְיָבֹא, וְיַגִּיעַ, וְיֵרָאֶה, וְיֵרָצֶה וְ...

ךְ: וְזִכְרוֹן יְרוּשָׁלַיִם זִכְרוֹנֵנוּ וּפִקְדוֹנֵנוּ וְזִכְרוֹן אֲבוֹתֵינוּ. וְזִכְרוֹן מָשִׁיחַ בֶּן דָּוִד עַבְדֶ...

לְטוֹבָה לְחֵן וּלְחֶסֶד עִיר קָדְשֶׁךָ. וְזִכְרוֹן כָּל עַמְּךָ בֵּית יִשְׂרָאֵל לְפָנֶיךָ. לִפְלֵטָה...

אֱלֹהֵינוּ בּוֹ לְטוֹבָה וּלְרַחֲמִים לְחַיִּים וּלְשָׁלוֹם בְּיוֹם חַג הַמַּצּוֹת הַזֶּה. זָכְרֵנוּ יְיָ...

THE JEWISH KITCHEN

THE JEWISH KITCHEN

by Alena Krekulová and Jana Doležalová

Consultant editor Judy Jackson

CHARTWELL
BOOKS, INC.

Designed and produced by Aventinum Publishing House,
Prague, Czech Republic

Original text by Alena Krekulová and Jana Doležalová
English text edited by Penelope Cream
Consultant editor Judy Jackson
Photographs by Antonín Braný, Dana Cabanová and Rudolf Sokol
Illustrations by Helena Pěkná
Graphic design by Věra Běťáková

English text © The Promotional Reprint Company Limited 1996
© AVENTINUM NAKLADATELSTVÍ, s.r.o., 1996

This edition published 1996 by The Promotional Reprint Company
Limited for

CHARTWELL BOOKS, INC.
A Division of BOOK SALES, INC.
P.O. BOX 7100
EDISON, NEW JERSEY, 08818 - 7100

Printed in Slovak Republic
ISBN 0 7858 0639 3
3/99/80/51-01

PUBLISHER'S NOTE
Every effort has been made by the publisher to ensure that
permission to use quoted material has been obtained from the
copyright holders. In the event of any questions arising as to
the use of this material such questions should be addressed to
Aventinum Publishing House, Prague, Czech Republic.

CONTENTS

INTRODUCTION

This Jewish cookbook is not a cookery book in the usual sense because the recipes and culinary tradition have been set against a religious and historical background. In fact, a book on Jewish cuisine could not be presented in any other way. This is because, for the Jewish people, the preparation and consumption of food is as much a religious ritual as a prayer. This activity is sacred in Judaism. It is made sacred by performing it in harmony with the orders contained in the principles of Jewish ritual cooking – *kashrut*. This is discussed in the first chapter of the book. This spiritual and religious aspect is particularly evident during Jewish festivals. Festive banquets are part of a religious rite where every food has hidden meaning and symbolism. The best example of this is given by the main liturgy at Passover, which is not performed in synagogue but at home at the festive table where the dishes and drinks play as important a role as the spoken word.

Although there is a strong focus on religious aspects in *The Jewish Kitchen*, the book is not exclusively for devout Jews. The main objective is to offer everyone interested in Jewish culture a taste of the wisdom, spiritualism and beauty of the Jewish world which has been threatened in Europe by the events of the twentieth century, but, in spite of all this, still survives. The work of Jewish writers and the countless rituals, customs and traditions passed down from generation to generation have kept the Jewish culture alive. In this book, the origins and meanings of each festival are complemented by excerpts from Jewish literature. This includes how the Sabbath was kept at Sighet, a town where Elie Wiesel was born, and how Purim was celebrated in Warsaw, where Isaac Bashevis Singer spent his youth. The unique world of Hassidic leaders and their disciples is described by Martin Buber and Jiří Langer. These stories present a deep and accurate insight into the Jewish soul.

The recipes featured in this book are part of a rich legacy from the past. They come from every corner of the world where Jews have found refuge throughout the Diaspora. The variety of Jewish festive cuisine has undoubtedly been moulded by the culinary traditions of the regions that have become home to Jews around the world. Guided by the instructions and laws of the rabbinical authorities, Jewish housewives used their skill to adapt local customs and produce. This has resulted in a vast wealth of different foods, each of which has a history all of its own, which is usually so complicated and interesting that it could make a book by itself. This book concentrates on the cuisine of the Ashkenazi Jews – challah, gefilte fish, latkes, kugel, and kreplach – to name but a few. Each name is a legend in itself. These dishes are the bonds which unite Jews with their ancestors and with other Jews around the world. They are one of the essential parts of the Jewish faith and cultural identity. This book presents the background to the most popular, traditional Jewish recipes and acquaints the reader with their symbolism and tradition. For some readers this may be a nostalgic return to the times of their childhood, while for others this may be a new experience.

*Shiviti table, Bohemia,
1821*

*Passover Haggadah, blessing
over wine and food,
Moravia, 1728*

KASHRUT – THE DIETARY LAWS OF JEWISH RITUAL COOKING
כשרות

Left:
Ritual slaughter or shechitah, Italy, 1435

Nutrition experts using scientific methods to examine healthy eating are coming to the conclusions already known from the Torah that the way we live affects our spiritual and emotional life. The fact that food becomes a part of the body has a clear effect on the soul, which forms an inseparable union with it. Bad nutrition has an unfavourable effect on the spirit and character of man at every stage of his life. In short: you are what you eat. It is this simple and yet important truth which had given rise to the laws of Jewish ritual cooking. *Kashrut* is a diet for the body as much as the soul. Both were given to man by God, and the Torah teaches us how to treat both these gifts correctly. Observing *kashrut* means helping to develop and intensify the harmonious coexistence of the soul and body; the body then ceases to be a mere instrument for satisfying the basic necessities of life that we have in common with animals, and instead becomes a dignified dwelling place for the soul.

At least 50 of the 613 of God's commandments deal with food and setting the table and serving. The observance of these commandments is an integral part of the everyday life of Jews. It is a bond which reinforces their solidarity and the feeling of mutual roots in a jointly created tradition. What is the point of these complicated and, at first sight, almost incomprehensible commandments, and why are they as important today as they were during the time of our ancestors? The kitchen for Jews is not just a place where food is prepared; it is, above all, the spiritual centre of their household. The observance of the dietary laws is but one of many ways of achieving the consecration of daily life. The fulfilment of *mitzvot*, God's commandments, means raising up even such an ordinary act as preparing and eating food in service to God. The purpose of *kashrut*, together with a whole number of other commandments concerning everyday life, helps to bridge the dualism between the physical and the spiritual, the ordinary and the sacred. An ordinary act is transformed into a sacred ritual through which man is purified and comes into close contact with God. That is why the statements in the Torah relating to the laws of *kashrut* contain the concepts of the sacrament and consecration. So it is written in the Book of Leviticus: "I am the Lord your God, ye shall therefore sanctify yourselves, and ye shall be holy: for I am holy" (Lev. Chap. 11:44).

The Talmud, the book of oral laws, compares a Jewish household to a small temple, the set table to the sacrificial altar. Just as the sacrifice laid on the altar had to correspond to the complicated ritual laws, so the food laid on the table at home must not only taste and smell good, but must also be prepared precisely in accordance with the laws of Jewish ritual cooking. Sitting at a table and sharing a meal involves sacred duties, full of hidden meanings and symbols. Each detail has its own place and purpose so each day the fascinating and unique atmosphere which prevails over a table set for a Jewish meal can be created. Every day Jews all over the world wash their hands before taking bread and sprinkling salt on it as the Jewish priests used to do in the Temple. Every day they bless the bread and every day they end their meal with a prayer of thanksgiving. The sanctity of the act of receiving food every day is clearly expressed by the words of Rabbi Simeon who said that if three (men) sit at a table and none utter a single word from the Torah, it is as if they eat from sacrifices of the dead; but three that eat on one table and do say words of Torah over it, it is as though they eat from God's table. (Ethics of the Fathers, Chap. 3.)

The main laws of *kashrut* differentiate between "clean" and "unclean" animals, with

Slaughterhouse, kitchen and dining-room, Spain, c. 1330

only the former considered edible. Further laws, such as the requirement of ritual slaughter (*shechitah*), the ban on consuming blood and the consistent separation of dairy products from meat food are all motivated by a profound respect for the life of God's creatures. Only God can give and take life. When God created people, the food he chose for them was "every herb bearing seed, which is upon the face of all the earth, and every tree on which is the fruit of a tree yielding seed" (Gen. Chap. 29). The first people were in fact vegetarians and remained so until the days of Noah and his descendants (Gen. Chap. 9:1–4), when they were allowed to obtain food by killing animals. This concession expresses the need for compromise between the ideal and real conditions of life. Man sinned and was driven out of Paradise to begin life again in a real world where the ideal state of harmony which existed in the Garden of Eden no longer applied. So human beings started to act in ways which were incompatible with the basic principles of Judaism. How is man to preserve his respect for life if he is justified in taking the life of other beings? How is he to exalt the sinful and reprehensible act of killing into a respectable deed which does not blemish his soul and does not oppose God's commandments?

The killing of animals was always regarded in Judaism as a concession by God to man. So, man must have been aware of the seriousness of such an act and was able to carry full responsibility for it in the face of the Creator and life itself. In principle he was not supposed to kill without reason, for sport or for satisfying his aggressive instincts, but only when requiring meat essential to his nourishment. There is a strict ban on hunting with a weapon and it is by no means a coincidence that Nimrod, the mythical founder of Babylon, was, in Judaism, considered one of the embodiments of evil. Likewise, Jews never used fishing tackle but caught fish in nets.

Jews are only allowed to eat the meat of an animal killed by ritual slaughter, *shechitah*. The meat of animals which have died a natural death, or have been killed by another animal, is not regarded as kosher, nor is meat from animals that have been ill.

Ritual slaughter or shechitah, Spain, 1320–1330

Apart from bringing the quickest and least painful death to animals, *shechitah* is also of deep religious significance. Its roots date back to biblical times when Jews were allowed to eat only meat of animals which had been offered in sacrifice to God. In this way the unclean act of killing was purified and consecrated by being incorporated within the bounds of ritual sacrifice. This tradition disappeared, but the need for a purifying ritual persisted and was fulfilled by the ritual form of slaughter. *Shechitah* transforms the slaughter of animals into a religious rite of deep importance, reminding Jews of the sanctity of life which can be removed only in a certain manner and under certain conditions. The requirement of humane slaughter gave rise to the special profession of *shochet*, or slaughterer, authorized to kill cattle and poultry in accordance with the laws of *kashrut*. This demanding work can be carried out only by a skilful and experienced man who lives an impeccable life and upholds all God's commandments.

The Book of Leviticus says: "For the life of the flesh is in the blood" (meaning that blood is the principal carrier of life). "Therefore I said unto the children of Israel: No soul of you shall eat blood" (Lev. Chap. 17:11). For this reason meat should not be served unless all the blood has been removed from it (see Meat food). Perhaps the best known law of *kashrut*, expressed in the verse "Thou shalt not seethe a kid in his mother's milk" (Deut. Chap. 14:11), was not upheld originally. From the description of the first feast in biblical history, it is known that the three angels who visited Abraham were honoured with meal cakes and a calf which was served with cream and milk. In the course of time, however, the commandment for the consistent separation of meat from milk was extended to the direct consumption of food so that milk dishes could not be eaten simultaneously with meat, but only after a certain time had elapsed. The word *kosher* means "fit", "proper", and is generally applied to foods that meet the requirements of the dietary laws, i.e. *kashrut*. The opposite of kosher is *terefah* which literally means "a torn animal". Originally this term was used to describe the meat of

בָּשָׂר

kosher animals killed by being torn apart by other animals or which had died a natural death. In the broader sense of the word it encompasses all non-kosher foodstuffs and such methods of preparation which oppose the rules of *kashrut*.

HOW TO RUN A KOSHER HOUSEHOLD

Kosher and terefah

The following animals fulfil the requirements of *kashrut*: ruminant animals with cleft hooves, i.e. cattle, goats, sheep, deer, gazelles and antelopes; also poultry – geese, ducks, hens, turkey hens and cocks, pheasants, partridges, quails and pigeons. Among the forbidden species are pigs, donkeys, horses, camels, rodents, carnivores and water mammals. All fishes with fins and scales can be eaten; however, the shark, ray, sturgeon (including caviar), eel and predatory fishes are not considered kosher. Also forbidden are reptiles, amphibians, molluscs, crustaceans (including oysters, crabs, lobsters) and insects, apart from four species of locust which are still eaten by some Jews in the Orient.

Meat, milk and parve

All dishes in Jewish cooking belong to one of three basic categories: meat, milk and parve (neutral food).

Meat food

All meat and meat products must come from animals slaughtered according to the regulations of *shechitah*. Before cooking, all the blood must be removed from the meat by koshering. If meat purchased at the butcher's is not processed in this way, it has to be made kosher at home. The procedure is as follows: rinse the meat thoroughly and submerge it in a saucepan of water for at least half an hour. This saucepan must not be used for any other purpose. Remove the meat from the water, lay it out on a board full of holes so that the blood can flow out and sprinkle the entire surface with salt (use coarse salt so that it does not dissolve too quickly). Allow the blood to trickle away for 1–2 hours. Finally rinse the meat thoroughly three times under running water. Bones covered in meat are made kosher in the same way as the meat. Put aside bones without meat so that no blood drips on them.

Kosher board, Bohemia, mid-19th century

Poultry

If the poultry is not cleaned, remove all the giblets before it is made kosher and open the gullet. Clean the stomach and cut the cusp off the heart to release the blood that has collected inside. Place aside the liver as this is made kosher in a different way. The same procedure is used as with meat to make the flesh, the heart and stomach kosher. If eggs are found in the poultry, peel off the membrane and make them kosher well away from the other meat so that they do not come into contact with the blood.

Liver cannot be made kosher in the usual way because it contains too much blood, so it should be grilled. Rinse the liver thoroughly, cut it up and sprinkle it with salt. Grill on each side until the liver changes colour. The liver is then koshered and is ready for further cooking.

Dairy food

This encompasses milk and all dairy products. The milk must come from a kosher animal. The foodstuff in question must not contain any non-kosher ingredients nor any animal fat.

Separating meat from milk

The commandment for the separation of meat from milk applies to both the consumption of food and its preparation. Milk and meat foods must not be mixed together in a single dish. Special care must be given to bread and pastries and various desserts. Always carefully examine what ingredients they are made with so that a dish containing butter or milk is not served at the same time as meat. Milk dishes may only be eaten at certain time after the consumption of a meat dish. This usually varies from 3 to 6 hours, according to local tradition. However, a meat dish can be served after a milk dish without a break. A prayer should be said after the dairy food, the mouth should be rinsed and the table-cloth changed. Nonetheless, even in such cases it is customary to wait for half an hour to an hour.

A kosher kitchen must contain two sets of pots and pans: one set is used for preparing meat and the other for the milk dishes. In practice this can be done in various ways, e.g. the sets of pots and pans can differ in colour or be marked with the letters F and M (the first letters of the Yiddish words *fleishig* [flesh] and *milchig* [milk]). Two sets of washing-up sponges and tea-towels are required and must also be kept separate. Pots and pans for milk and meat dishes may not be washed together either, so it is best

Kosher kitchen tools,
Spain, early 14th century

to have two separate sinks. Refrigerators may be used to store all kinds of dishes; however, within them, permanent separate places must be reserved for both milk and meat foods.

Parve (pareve, pareveh)

This term describes foodstuffs which contain neither meat nor milk. These include kosher fish, eggs, fruit, vegetables, mushrooms, cereals, pasta, pulses, bread and certain kinds of desserts and drinks.

Parve food may form a part of both meat and milk dishes, with the exception of fish which may not be cooked or served together with meat. Parve dishes are therefore considered to be either meat or milk foods and so are prepared in the appropriate set of pots and pans. Nevertheless, if prepared separately (e.g. baking cakes), it is customary to have separate pots for parve too. Fruit and vegetables do not require any special preparation, but must be thoroughly washed and examined for worms or bugs. The same applies to flour, sugar, salt, herbs and spices. Eggs must be examined to make sure they do not contain embryos or blood spots; if these are found the egg cannot be consumed.

We kept the food kosher for a long time, mainly thanks to Mrs Julie, a devout Catholic who, as a young girl, served for our devout Jewish aunt and then observed the dietary as well as other laws of Jewish religion in our home.

Since time immemorial, fish was a popular dish in Jewish cuisine. Hence, the preparation of a fish course for the kosher menu resulted in a number of excellent recipes. The consumption of fish was always associated with the celebration of Saturday, therefore it had to be part of at least one course.

FRANTIŠEK LANGER, *Recollections*

Many times a day Yoine Meir repeated the words of the rabbi that man may not be more merciful than the fount of all compassion. The Torah states that you shall kill of your own herd and flock, as commanded by Me.

Moses was instructed by God on Mount Sinai about the ways in which to avoid all uncleanliness when slaughtering and opening up animals. All this is the mystery of mysteries – life, death, man and animal. Those who are not killed die of various sicknesses and often suffer for long weeks or months. In the forest one animal eats another. In the sea one fish swallows another. No one can escape the sentries of this world.

Despite this, Yoine Meir found no consolation. Each quiver of the poultry being slaughtered made his guts turn. The killing of each animal, whether big or small, caused him as much pain as if he were cutting his own throat. Of all the punishments he would have had to endure, making something kosher was the worst.

ISAAC BASHEVIS SINGER, *The Kosher Man*

Modche brought an enormous stone pot with two handles and a basket topped with flour from the pantry. He placed the basket on the table but held the pot indecisively in both hands.

"I don't know about that pot, Joseph...," he stated with embarrassment.

"What don't you know?"

"I don't know whether it is a meat or a milk one."

"You must know what Rezi cooks in it."

"I do, plum jam. But I don't know if plum jam is a meat or milk dish. What do you think, Joseph?"

"I think it's all an evil," surmised Shpanek.

"Anyway, she won't know anything."

"I'm not so much concerned about Rezi as I am about God," admitted Modche.

"You don't still believe in such things! God remembers Sedletín once every Hungarian moon, and He has other things to worry about here than Rezi's pot."

"You wouldn't dare talk like that in front of Rezi," doubted Modche.

"I would," Shpanek assured him, "and what is more, I would tell Rezi that God couldn't care less about her pot. And whether it is a milk or a meat one, just put it down and let's get on with it."

"Let it be your sin if it isn't the right pot," Modche insured himself for all instances and placed the pot on the table.

VOJTĚCH RAKOUS, *Modche and Rezi*

Well, first of all something about this pleasant commandment. It is the commandment of rinsing the hands. This is done in the following way: pour clean water into a mug. However, make sure that this cup has no flaws. Do not, for instance, pour the water into a flower pot! That has a hole in the bottom.

Likewise, there must not be a single nick on the edge of the mug. Its edge must be as straight as the kosher knife. Pick up the mug with the water in your right hand, pass the mug from your right to your left hand and with your left hand empty half the water onto the right hand. Take the mug from your right hand and with your right hand pour the remaining water onto your left hand. Rub your hands together, then thank the Lord God for "blessing us with his commandments and ordering us to wash our hands", whereupon we then wipe our dear hands properly, as throughout this holy ceremony we should have a towel thrown over our left shoulder. A proper Hasid never carries just a handkerchief in his pocket, but always a towel as well. When wiping your hands always keep the left hand covered with this towel. Not everyone knows this, but it is very important. Only after we have washed our hands this way and have really thoroughly and conscientiously wiped them can we finally bless the bread and eat it.

JIŘÍ LANGER, *Nine Gates*

If you do not wash your hands before eating in accordance with the law, then you expose yourself to the terrible danger that, as the Talmud writes, happened to one guest and serves as a warning to all.

This man came to an inn and asked for a meal. The innkeeper noticed that the guest had not washed his hands before eating bread and assumed that he was not a Jew but some Greek or Aramean, in short, a pagan. So he served him with a meal of pork and cabbage. The terrible mistake was not discovered until after the meal.

From this it can be seen how each sin leads to a second and even bigger sin.

JIŘÍ LANGER, *Nine Gates*

My lame grandfather was not an expert in the Talmud but was well versed in the religious laws and observed all the sabbaths and feast days. He and Grandmother still observed the strict laws of keeping the milk and meat dishes separate – and Father would smile when he talked of this. He and Aunt Emily would spend the feasts in their native Slavětín and Grandfather and Grandmother would leave and cross the Podblanické field to get to Lukavec where there was a Czech prayerhouse Or Tomidu, as of 1871, so they could take part in the services. Young student Alfred and Aunt Emily roasted a chicken and put butter in it! They did not tell their parents anything until Grandfather had finished with the last bone ... and it was then that both the devout repatriates found out why they found it so tasty. The religiously indifferent children had breached the law on the separation of meat from milk and on a feast day at that! So a heavy clout followed.

FRANZ KAFKA, *My Limping Grandfather*

Drapery, Bohemia,
19th century

THE CALENDAR
לוח

The Jewish calendar, *luach hashana*, is based on the lunar cycle. Due to the fact that the moon revolves round the earth in $29\frac{1}{2}$ days, the normal year is made up of 12 months and each month, or *chodesh*, alternately has 29 or 30 days. This represents 354 days in a year. The Bible decrees that the feast of Passover be celebrated in spring, so the lunar calendar has to be adjusted to the solar system by $365\frac{1}{4}$ days every year. This is done by adding an extra 29-day month (*Adar Sheni*) – this occurs seven times every 19 solar years. Another adjustment of the calendar is that the months of Cheshvan and Kislev are made longer or shorter by one day. This takes place because neither Yom Kippur (the Day of Atonement) nor Hoshana Rabba (the seventh day of Succot) must fall on the Sabbath.

Each month begins with a new moon. *Rosh Chodesh* (literally, "head of the month") was an important feast in biblical times, mainly celebrated with the bringing of special Temple sacrifices. Up to the reform of the calendar in the mid-fourth century CE (Common Era) the beginning of a month was set by direct observation. At least two witnesses had to confirm that the moon had appeared and on the basis of their evidence the Supreme Council, the Sanhedrin, designated the beginning of the month by which the dates of the various feast were fixed. Then messengers would travel across the Holy Land and its closest environs declaring the exact date of the new moon. However, Jews living in the most distant lands of the Diaspora were exposed to the danger of not finding out the precise date of a feast in time, therefore they would celebrate a feast for two days. Despite the fact that these reasons have long since passed, this custom has survived and still applies to certain feasts. If a month has 30 days, *Rosh Chodesh* is celebrated for two days: the first day falls on the thirtieth day of the month and the second day on the first day of the subsequent month. If a month has 29 days, *Rosh Chodesh* is celebrated on the first day of the new month.

The first month of the civic and religious calendar is considered to be the month of Nisan. It was in this month that the Jews were led out of Egypt – "This month shall be unto you the beginning of months..." (Ex. Chap. 12:2). *Rosh Hashanah*, the New Year, is celebrated on the first two days of the seventh month, Tishri. It is then (from the New Year) that the years of the creation of the world are counted.

The months of the Jewish calendar are: Nisan (30 days), Iyar (29 days), Sivan (30 days), Tamuz (29 days), Av (30 days), Elul (29 days), Tishri (30 days), Cheshvan (29 or 30 days), Kislev (29 or 30 days), Tevet (29 days), Shevat (30 days) and Adar (29 days). In a leap year Adar has 30 and Adar Sheni 29 days.

In the Hebrew calendar a day lasts from twilight to twilight according to the words of the Book of Genesis: "And the evening and the morning were, one day" (Gen. Chap. 1:5). A week consists of seven days called, in order, the "first day" (*yom rishom*), "second day" (*yom sheni*) etc. and ending with the seventh day, the Sabbath.

The Jewish feast days are divided into two groups: those which were set down in the Torah, which are the High Holy Days and the feasts of pilgrimage, and those religious festivals and fast days introduced at a later period which recall various historical events. The High Holy Days – *yamim nora'im* – are *Rosh Hashanah*, which is celebrated on the first

Left:
Synagogue clock, Bohemia, c. 1870

Scales of justice, Calendar, Bohemia, 18th century

and second day of the month of Tishri, and Yom Kippur which falls on the tenth day of the same month. The festivals of pilgrimage – Passover (Pesach), Shavuot and Sukkot, including Shemini Atseret and Simchat Torah – are celebrated to recall the important turning points in the history of Israel. These are the agricultural feasts connected with harvest festivals. Their Hebrew name is *Shalosh Regalim* – "Three times thou shalt keep feast unto me in the year" (Ex. Chap. 23:14). *Regalim* has two meanings. Apart from "times", it also means "feet" and this is where the idea of pilgrimage, walking feasts, originates, it was a time when the Israelite men were to appear before the Lord on a designated site. During the time of the Temple, a great number of pilgrims came to Jerusalem bringing prescribed sacrifices to the sanctuary.

The festival days of Chanukah and Purim appeared in post-biblical times, the happiest feast days of the year. Both recall the victory of the Jews over their enemies.

Other historical religious feast days include that of Lag b'Omer falling on the 18th of Iyar which recalls the uprising of Bar Kochba against the Roman oppressors in the second century CE. It was also on this day that the terrible plague which broke out among the pupils of Rabbi Akiba came to a miraculous end. That is why this day is

*Calendar, Bohemia,
18th century*

celebrated as the "feast of scholars". This feast is also connected with the name of Rabbi Simeon ben Jochai, the author of the Zohar, who, according to tradition, died on this day. Each year in Israel, even today, a pilgrimage takes place to his grave in Meron.

Another feast day is Tu bishvat – the New Year of Trees – which is celebrated on the 15th day of the month of Shevat signifying the beginning of spring in Israel. The most significant of the fast days and days of mourning is Tishah b'Av; this is the saddest day of the Jewish calendar and recalls the destruction of the first and second Temples and the other tragic events which occurred on this day.

*Zodiac with Hebrew
months*

Dates of the feasts

ROSH HASHANAH 1st and 2nd of Tishri
   (September–October)
YOM KIPPUR 10th of Tishri (September–October)
SUKKOT 15th–21st of Tishri (September–
   October)
SHEMINI ATSERET 22nd of Tishri (September–
   October)
SIMCHAT TORAH 23rd of Tishri (September–
   October) 22nd of Tishri in Israel
CHANUKAH from 25th of Kislev for 8 days
   (December–January)
TU BISHVAT 15th of Shevat (January–February)
PURIM 14th of Adar (February–March)
   15th of Adar in Israel
PASSOVER 15th–22nd of Nisan (March–April)
   15th–21st of Nisan in Israel
LAG B'OMER 18th of Iyar (April–May)
SHAVUOT 6th and 7th of Sivan (May–June)
   6th of Sivan in Israel
TISHAH B'AV 9th of Av (July–August)

בָּרוּךְ אַתָּה יְיָ אֱלֹהֵינוּ מֶלֶךְ הָעוֹלָם
שֶׁהֶחֱיָנוּ וְקִיְּמָנוּ וְהִגִּיעָנוּ לַזְּמַן הַזֶּה ׃

צוּרַת הַצַּיָּד צוֹדֶה הָאַרְנֶבֶת עִם כְּלָבִים ׃   וְהַיּוֹחֵר תּוֹפְשׂוֹ בַּעֲקַבְוֹ ׃
וְהִיא צוֹעֶקֶת בְּמַר נֶפֶשׁ מְנַחֲמֶיהָ הִדְרִיכוּנִי   צוֹן קָצְבִי יִסְבּוּנִי ׃

כַּשֹּׁעַל שָׁבוּעוֹת בְּמוֹצָאֵי שַׁבָּת אֶתְחִיל כֵּן

בָּרוּךְ אַתָּה יְיָ אֱלֹהֵינוּ מֶלֶךְ
הָעוֹלָם בּוֹרֵא פְּרִי הַגֶּפֶן ׃
בָּרוּךְ אַתָּה יְיָ אֱלֹהֵינוּ מֶלֶךְ
הָעוֹלָם אֲשֶׁר בָּחַר בָּנוּ

SABBATH
שבת

"And God blessed the seventh day and sanctified it: because on it He had rested from all His work which He created and made" (Gen. Chap. 2:3). And we, the people, also bless it as we were created in God's image. "Remember the Sabbath day, to keep it holy," states the eighth commandment. Every week we stray from the course of life to celebrate the day of rest for the body and soul, an island of sanctity and blessing in the sea of ordinary days.

Work is strictly prohibited on the Sabbath. What is meant by work in this context is any sort of intentionally creative activity such as making a fire, carrying loads, writing, and many other activities including travelling. A precise definition of prohibited work is found in the Talmudic tractate on the Sabbath. The ban on all creative work releases us from the grip of the surrounding world. One day a week we stop dominating and influencing the world. We consciously surrender our control over it and submit to the will of God to remind ourselves that God is the creator of the world and is the sole true Lord and Master. However, rest does not mean inactivity. "Call the Sabbath a delight," proclaims Isaiah (Is. Chap. 58:13). *Oneg Sabbat*, rejoicing in the Sabbath includes three special Sabbath feasts (the *seudot*), festive clothes, a purifying bath in a *mikvah* (bath house), the lighting of the Sabbath candles, the Kiddush recited over wine and, above all, plenty of time for devout meditation and the study of the Torah. According to Talmudic tradition, every Jew receives an extra soul on the Sabbath and this Sabbath soul enables him to study the Torah

Left and right:
*Sabbath songs and blessing,
Bohemia (Prague), 1514*

The Sabbath table

with greater keenness and understanding than at any other time. It is on the Sabbath that all the ordinary worries and anxieties are forgotten. We put aside all the usual thoughts which tie us down and distract us from the substantial matter of life. We find ourselves in another time dimension. We stop in the middle of the road to pull ourselves together and become purified. It is on this day that we are closer to God and to ourselves.

It is a Friday afternoon, the preparations for the Sabbath are culminating. A feverish rush of activity lasts until the very last minute. Finally everything has been bought and is prepared.

A pot with food stands on the stove prepared for the following day of rest. In carefully polished candlesticks, candles wait to be lit by the woman of the household to welcome the holy Sabbath. Everything is clean and gleaming. There is an atmosphere of joyous expectation. "Come, my Beloved, to greet the bride – the Sabbath presence, let us welcome the Queen of the Sabbath!" are the words of the famous mystical song composed by Rabbi Alkabea. The desired moment has arrived, the Sabbath has begun. For a Jewish woman, lighting Sabbath candles to welcome its arrival is the most honoured of all her obligations. The candles are lit in the last half-hour before the stars appear, but usually about a quarter of an hour before sundown. This is so that some time from the weekday is added to the holy day. At least two candles are normally lit. This number corresponds to the two words by which the Torah commands us to observe Sabbath: "remember" and "keep" (Ex. Chap. 20:8, Deut. Chap. 5:12).

However, usually each child in a family has his or her own Sabbath candle. After lighting a candle the woman warms her hands over the flame and covers her eyes. Then she gently recites a blessing and prays for the good of her loved ones. The roots

Hymns and psalms,
Moravia, 1813

of this traditional ritual date back to earliest biblical times. Sarah lit the Sabbath candles, and the tent in which she lived with Abraham remained illuminated throughout
the week until the beginning of the next Sabbath. After her death, the light went out

*Book of benediction,
Bohemia (Prague), 1514*

and returned the moment Isaac's wife Rebecca began to light the Sabbath candles. All Jewish women rejoice in lighting them and do so with love to this day. The Torah is compared to light and each one of its commandments is compared to a candle. The erect flame of a candle lights up the soul and raises it to God. The flames of the Sabbath candles fill our homes with the light of the Torah and bring happiness and God's blessing to the whole family.

"Shabbat shalom! Shabbat shalom!" is how mothers and children greet one another. "Shabbat shalom!" reply the fathers returning from the synagogue. They are so elated and inspired with the spirit of Sabbath that they are supposed to be accompanied by two angels, one good and one evil. If everything is properly prepared for

*Challah cover, Bohemia,
late 19th century*

the celebration of the Sabbath, then the words of the good angel will no doubt apply for the next Sabbath, which are "May it be the same next Shabbat!" However, in the case of a poorly prepared Sabbath, the same words will ensure that the evil angels' influence over the Sabbath will win out next time. A song of greeting addressed to these angels preceeds the Kiddush, or blessing over the wine, on Friday night.

Sabbath supper

The table has been laid and the home feast may begin. On a starched snowy white tablecloth are two loaves of bread covered with a decoratively embroidered cloth; there is also a goblet for the blessing of the wine, a knife for the bread and a pot for the salt. The warming and flickering flames of the Sabbath candles gleam silently in the twilight. Sacred peace and tranquility radiate everywhere. Everyone is happy and glad to be able to share their happiness with their loved ones. Purified of all the ordinary everyday matters, they sit down to the sacred ritual of the first Sabbath feast. The father blesses the children, and in praise of his wife, he utters the following words from the Book of Proverbs: "Who can find a virtuous woman? For her price is far above rubies. The heart of her husband doth safely trust in her, so that he shall have no need of spoil" (Prov. Chap. 31:10–11). He then lifts up the cup and recites the blessing over the wine: "Blessed art thou, O Lord our God, King of the universe, who createst the fruit of the vine." Everyone at the table drinks from this cup. This is followed by the ritual washing of the hands and the blessing of the bread. "Blessed art thou, O Lord our God, King of the universe, who bringest forth food (bread) from the earth," says the father and gives each of those

present a piece of *challah* dipped in salt. Wine and bread were already regarded in biblical times as the symbols of the gift of the earth and played an important role in Temple ritual. They form an integral part of the Sabbath table which is seen as a reminder of the altar in the temple. The two loaves of *challah* also symbolize the double portion of manna which the Lord used to send down to our ancestors in the wilderness so they would not have to look for food on the day of rest. (Ex. Chap. 16:2–30) Wine drives away sorrow and lifts the spirit and so helps to bring joy on the Sabbath. All food strengthens not only the body but also the soul. For the Sabbath this is doubly true.

The Sabbath feast lasts a long time. Everyone feels free and relaxed, no one is in a hurry to get anywhere. A lively discussion takes place at the table but if possible worldly matters are not talked about. Passages from the previous week's Torah reading are discussed and commandments, habits and customs are explained; great figures and events from Jewish history are recalled. Children ask questions and adults answer them. There is also a lot of singing. There are countless Sabbath songs or Zemirot. Their words are found in Psalms, in prayer books and in many other holy scriptures. Whether they are long or short, the melodies simple or very complicated, they all intensify and deepen the feeling of joy and happiness which fills everyone's hearts of these festive occasions.

The Sabbath morning service begins later than a service on a week day. It culminates in the reading of the week's portion of the Torah, the *sidrah*, to which the sermon given by the rabbi, the *derasha,* is usually related. After the service the worshippers return to their homes and the time for dinner draws near. A calm and festive mood reigns, without any hustle and bustle. No cooking has to be done as the pot of savoury cholent has been kept warm in the oven. Also called schollet, this is the traditional Sabbath delicacy made of beans or peas and barley, flavoured with goose or turkey meat.

The dinner takes place in the same way as the *seuda* on the eve of Sabbath. Then there is a whole afternoon to look forward to full of rejoicing in the Sabbath. Some people prefer to stay at home and spend the time resting, meditating or studying,

Above and right:
Cups for the Kiddush,
Bohemia, 2nd half
of the 19th century

Festival plate, Palestine,
early 20th century

while others prefer to enjoy themselves in the company of friends. In the early evening the worshippers gather together again in the synagogue to say *minchah* (the afternoon prayer) and eat the third Sabbath meal, *seuda shlishit*. It is the least abundant of the meals but is no less festive. It cannot be omitted because, as is written in the Talmud (Sabbath 118 A), he who observes the commandment of the three sabbatical meals will receive a rich reward in the next world. It is getting dark slowly. The Sabbath is coming to an end. As soon as the first three stars appear, the evening prayers, *ma'ariv*, are said. The last part of the Sabbath service, *motzei Shabbat*, the departure of the Sabbath, begins with the words, "Let God give you of the dew of heaven".

A farewell is said to the Sabbath an hour after sunset with a beautiful symbolic ritual which is called *havdalah*. *Havdalah* means separation, and this ritual separates the festive day from the week days. A special *havdalah* candle is required, braided from several strands. The candle has several wicks whose flames join into one large strand. The honour of holding this torch falls upon the youngest boy in a family. "Behold God is my salvation in which I trust and I do not fear... I raise the Cup of Salvation and call upon the name of the Lord," prays the father who then recites the three blessings; over the wine, over the scented spices and over the flame of the *havdalah* candle. The scent of the spices, most often clove, is, according to tradition, a consolation for the departure of the Sabbath soul. The *havdalah* candle is the first light that can be lit after the Sabbath. It symbolizes the introductory act of creation, that is to say the words of the Lord: "Let there be light!" Then the father takes up the goblet and candle and says: "Blessed art thou, O Lord our God, king of the universe, who makest a distinction between week days and holy days, between Israel and other nations; and between the seventh day and the six days of work."

Havdalah candle holder,
Bohemia (Prague), 1820

The flame of the *havdalah* candle is then extinguished in the remaining wine. We wish each other "Shavua tov! Good week!" The holy Sabbath has come to an end, and we return to an ordinary week day. A new working week begins with a vision of the next Sabbath.

Above:
*Spice box, Slovakia,
late 18th century*

Right:
*Spice box, Bohemia,
late 18th century*

Below:
Havdalah, Spain, 1350–1360

Right:
The havdalah ceremony

Sighet. A Romanian, Hungarian, Austrian provincial town. It experienced Turkish, Russian and German occupation; all nations in this part of the world coveted this town. Despite the variety of languages which could be heard there and in spite of the difference in the governments which alternated, it was a Jewish town typical for this part of the region between the Carpathians and the Dnepr where there were hundreds, if not thousands. In view of the Jewish majority, there was purification before Yom Kippur, fasting at Tishah b'Av and lamentations over the destruction of the Temple, rejoicing and elation at the Rejoicing of the Law.

If you were to enter any of the streets on a Saturday, you would feel the presence of the Sabbath in the air. Closed shops. Not a living soul in the market places. The local office empty. For the Jews and their Christian neighbours it was a day of absolute rest. The old would depart for the study houses to listen to the words of the travelling preacher, the young strolled through the park, in the forest, by the river. Problems and cares could wait: Saturday was a refuge in time.

But on Friday afternoon, on the eve of the Sabbath, you could already feel it coming near. Men immersed themselves in the ritual bath so they could welcome it in. The women cleaned the houses, washed the floors, hurried with the cooking and dressed up in their nicest dresses. After returning from school, the boys would recite the Song of Songs. Later at the same time, the same song could be heard in all the houses: "Shalom aleichem malachei hashalom," blessed be the messengers of peace, come and enter in peace, oh angels of peace...

Rabbis and uneducated people, rich wholesalers and servants, employers and employees, all had the same words for the angels of the Sabbath which expressed the same gratitude.

"Who are the angels?" I once asked my grandfather whose chants excited me by their charm.

Instead of an answer, he leaned towards me and whispered a secret into my ear which I have kept to this day: "Dear boy, we are all angels, all of us who have gathered here full of sincerity and reconciliation around the table covered with a white tablecloth which has changed into an altar. You, I and all the other participants of the feast. It is here where the strength of the 'Sabbath' lies: by its effect man is constantly becoming more complete."

At that moment I heard the flap of celestial wings above my head, I really did hear it, I can swear by it. And throughout all this time that we, Grandfather, are apart, I have never again seen an angel, I also swear to that. I believe, Grandfather, that they remain hidden in our town in the mountains, just as invisible as you and I, as all of us.

ELIE WIESEL, *Return to Sighet*

During the Sabbath meal, the confidential and holy audience of the feast, the Hasidim sat silently at the table of Rabbi Volf and communicated with one another by modest gestures so as not to disturb the *tzaddik* engrossed in himself. At the house of Rabbi Volf it had, however, become a custom of his own will that everyone could, at any time, enter and sit at his table. It was so that now a man entered and sat down next to the others who made room for him, although they knew of his coarse ways. After a moment this man took a big radish out of his pocket, cut it up and began to chew it loudly. This was too much for his neighbours. "You glutton," they attacked him, "how dare you insult this distinguished table with your rough ways?" Although they tried to keep their voices down, the *tzaddik* noticed what was going on and said: "I've got a great appetite for a good radish. Could someone get me one?" The eater's face lit up with joy which removed and completely concealed his shame, and across the table he handed the Rabbi a handful of cut pieces of radish.

MARTIN BUBER, *Hasidic Tales, "The Radish Eater"*

There was a man who had unwittingly dishonoured the Sabbath because his cart had broken down. Although he had run with all his strength, he did not manage to reach the town before the beginning of the Sabbath, and for a penitence Rabbi Michael imposed a long fast on him. The man tried with all his strength to observe the fast, but he soon found that his body could not endure it and he fell ill and became depressed. Then he found out that the Bal Shem was travelling in the area and intended to stop off at one of the nearby towns. So he travelled after him, plucked up courage and asked him for something which would remove his sin. "Bring a pound of candles to the prayer house and have them lighted on the Sabbath," said the master. "This shall remove your sin." This man had the feeling that the Bal Shem had not heard him correctly – he repeated his concern laying greater stress on it. However, when the Bal Shem insisted on his unbelievably light verdict, he revealed the heavy penitence that Rabbi Michael had placed on him. "Do as I say," said the master, "and tell Rabbi Michael to come to the town of Chvostov where I wish to stay for the next Sabbath." With his face all lit up, the petitioner bade him farewell.

When Rabbi Michael was travelling to Chvostov, the wheel of his cart fell off and he had to go on foot the rest of the way. Although he hurried, he came to the town after nightfall, and as he was crossing the Bal Shem's threshold, he saw him standing erect taking a cup in his hand to bless the wine with the coming of the day of rest. The master interrupted his act and greeted the arrival: "Good Sabbath, man of ordinary sin! For as long as you had not felt the suffering of a sinner, you could not feel the dejection of his heart. Then how easily you could impose penitence on others! Good Sabbath, sinner!"

MARTIN BUBER, *Hasidic Tales, "Heavy Penitence"*

The devout Jew never considered God's law on the strict observance of the Sabbath as a day of rest as being some kind of commitment, but a beautiful gift from heaven to which he greatly looked forward week after week and for which he thanked the Lord in all his prayers. For it is on the Sabbath that he indulges in total respite.

He does not work, smoke, shave, go out for a drink nor look for entertainment. He sells nothing nor buys anything because he must not come into contact with money on the Sabbath. He prays and eats better than on a week day and treats himself to a short but sweet siesta after lunch.

It is a day of silence and peace. Even in families where no harmony reigns at other times, at least a truce is observed on the Sabbath.

E. KATZ, *Memories*

On Friday all the food was cooked for the Sabbath. The Sabbath was a day of rest. At the municipal house (in the church) there was a furnace where a dish was cooked called schollet – a mixture of barley and peas. The pot also contained bits of goose and it was a wonderful dish. At noon the furnace was opened up and everyone could carry off his own pot of food, and the schollet was still quite hot for serving at the table...

It is not suprising that we looked forward to Friday when Father would come home two hours early. He would prepare a six-branched hanging lamp. He would place in it a small wick made of cotton wool and pour in the oil. We all washed ourselves; Mother would wash the younger ones and we, the men of the house, would put on our best suits and go to synagogue. After synagogue our Father would bless us all, place both his hands on our heads and say the Hebrew blessing...

SIMON WELS, *At Bernat's*

I used to like going to the synagogue in Strakonice on a Friday evening. Cantor Menkes welcomed the Sabbath with a lively "Lecho Daudi", an ancient melody. None of the other melodies had changed either, including the one for the blessing of the wine. Of course there was also an ancient custom that afterwards Shammes Popper gave us, the boys, a taste of wine with a kind expression on his face – but we had to take the right sip otherwise we would get punished with a strict look in his eyes. The Friday evening meal at home began with the blessing of the sweetened *barches* covered in poppy seed. There were two *barches* – one was "adult" and one "a puppy" and I tried, though not always successfully, to claim it for myself. We always had noodle soup and a delicious veal roast.

After the service, the rest of the day was devoted to utter and profound rest and peace of the soul when our sorrows disappeared. Our fellow-believers armed us for the new week of work, problems and slightings. When the first star appeared in the sky, we lit the *havadalah* candle, a long multicoloured candle, plaited from thin strips like a girl's plait. We said farewell to the Sabbath. While the candle was submerged in a few drops of wine and slowly extinguished, and the believers took in the strengthening scent of the spices, an angel crept into the chamber to take away the crown of the Sabbath from the Jew straight after the prayer, the crown which he had just as invisibly and mysteriously set on his head on the Friday evening when the Jew had entered the prayer house. Another weekday had begun...

KAREL LAMBERK, *Memoirs*

Hanging candlestick,
Uzhgorod, 19th century

CHALLAH

No festive meal (with the exception of the feast of Passover) can begin without two loaves of *challah* on the table. The blessing which the father says before the meal over the *challah* and wine is one of the most beautiful of religious rituals, elevating the partaking of a meal together to a symbolic ceremony of thanksgiving. "Blessing" in Hebrew is *brachah* and this is the derivation of the word *barches*, the Ashkenazi term for the plaited bread.

The loaves of *challah* are a sign of the festive atmosphere and are an important symbol bonding us with our biblical ancestors and recalling the miracles which the Lord once worked for them. On the Sabbath the two loaves of *challah* represent the double portion of manna which the Lord sent down to the Israelites every Friday when they lived in the wilderness after leaving Egypt, so they would not have to pick and gather together the "heavenly bread" on the Sabbath. The manna remained fresh because it was covered with dew falling from the sky. To remind us of this miracle, two loaves symbolizing manna are placed between two napkins. When we look at the two loaves of *challah* on the Sabbath table, it makes us aware of God's mercy and the way he cares for us and satisfies all our needs, especially on the day of rest when we ourselves cannot do any work.

After the Kiddush or blessings over the wine, the father of the family raises both *challot* and makes the appropriate blessing. Then he cuts one of the loaves and gives everyone one small slice. Throughout the year it is the custom to dip its edge into salt, but on *Rosh Hashanah* it is dipped in honey for a good and sweet year.

Challah is baked in various shapes and sizes, from small loaves weighing only 3 oz to large 2 lb loaves. The traditional *challah* is plaited out of 6 or 12 strands of dough. It is here that there is another symbolic connection between *challah* and the Sabbath. The Torah describes the *mishkan*, the portable temple which served as a place of worship in the wilderness. It contained a cupboard for the scrolls on which were written the Ten Commandments, two altars and the menorah. There was also a table with 12 small open shelves onto which 12 loaves of bread were placed symbolizing the 12 tribes of Israel. It was always on the Friday that the Cohens, the priests who carried out the services in the *mishkan*, would bake 12 new loaves of bread replace the bread from the previous week. And although the loaves of bread to would lie on the shelves for the whole week, they were soft and warm as though freshly baked. The Sabbath *challah* recalls the miracle with the 12 loaves of bread which the Israelites experienced every week of their stay in the wilderness.

The *challah* which is baked on Rosh Hashanah is round. It symbolizes continuity without a beginning or an end because it is this time that we pray to the Lord for the continuity of life. On the eve of Yom Kippur *challah* is baked in the shape of a ladder, wings or raised arms so that our prayers and good deeds during the year are raised to the heavenly heights and are mercifully accepted.

A very important symbolic ritual, referring to Temple workship, is connected with the baking of the *challah*. The Torah writes: "Ye shall offer up a cake of the first of your dough for a heave offering: as ye do the heaven offering of the threshing floor, shall ye heave it" (Num. Chap. 15:20). In biblical times this commandment was fulfilled by putting aside part of the dough and giving it to the Cohen. Since the destruction of the Temple, Jewish women have fulfilled this in a symbolic form. If the dough weighs more than $3\frac{1}{2}$ lb, a piece of dough is taken away from it called *challah* which is then burned. This separation of *challah* is one of the three commandments which Jewish women are privileged and obliged to perform. By this act, they add a deeper spiritual dimension to the *challah* and also express their gratitude to the Lord for all the material possessions which He, in His generosity, presents to us.

Diagram of plaiting three lengths of challah

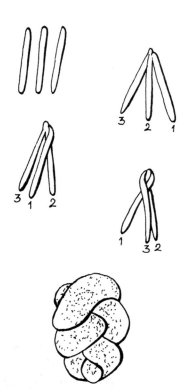

CHALLAH

Makes 2 loaves

$\frac{3}{4}$ oz fresh yeast or 3 level
  tsp dried yeast
$1\frac{1}{3}$ cup/11 fl oz warm
  water
1 tbsp sugar
3–5$\frac{1}{2}$ cups/1 lb 5 oz all
  purpose (plain) flour,
  sifted
1 tbsp salt
3 eggs, beaten
3 tbsp melted cooled
  butter or 3 tbsp oil, plus
  extra for greasing
1 egg yolk beaten with
  1 tsp water
poppy seed for sprinkling

Stir the yeast into the warm water, add the sugar and leave in a warm place. Meanwhile mix half of the flour with the beaten eggs and the butter or oil in a bowl. Pour in the dissolved yeast and gradually add the remaining flour and work into a firm dough. Place the dough on a floured board and knead for about 10 minutes. Then place it in a well-greased bowl, turn it over so that it is greased on both sides, cover with a cloth and leave in a warm place until it has risen to twice its size (this should take 1–2 hours). Preheat the oven to 400°F/Gas 6. Knead the risen dough for a few minutes and then braid the challah, using two lots of three strands of dough: divide the dough into six equal pieces. Form each piece into a roll of about 1 in in diameter and braid two challot, each from three strands. Place the challot on a greased baking tray at least 6 in away from one another, and leave them to rise in a warm place for another 10 minutes. Brush with the beaten egg yolk and water mixture and sprinkle with poppy seed. Bake for 35–45 minutes until golden.

CHOPPED LIVER

Serves 3 to 6

2 tbsp vegetable oil
2 onions, finely chopped
1 lb chicken livers
2 hard-boiled eggs, finely
  chopped
3 tbsp chicken fat
1 tsp salt
$\frac{1}{2}$ tsp ground black pepper

Heat the vegetable oil in a pan, add the onion and fry until browned. Remove the onion and fry the liver in the remaining fat for about 5 minutes. Mince the liver with the browned onion and hard-boiled eggs and then mash with the chicken fat, salt and pepper. Chill for 2 hours before serving.

MARINATED HERRING

Serves 6

3 large herrings
4 onions, sliced into thin
  rings
$\frac{1}{2}$ cup/4 fl oz wine vinegar
$\frac{3}{4}$ cup/6 fl oz water
2 tsp sugar

$\frac{1}{4}$ tsp chilli powder
$\frac{1}{2}$ tsp mustard seeds
7 black peppercorns
2 bay leaves
2 cloves
$\frac{3}{4}$ cup/6 fl oz soured
  cream

Leave the herrings to soak for at least 12 hours in cold water. Then wash in fresh water, remove the skin and bones and cut into several long pieces, each about 2 in in length. Layer these with the onion rings in a sealed container. Mix together the vinegar, water, sugar, herbs and spices in a pan, bring to the boil, then leave to cool. When cool pour over the herrings. Seal the container, shake several times and place in the refrigerator for 48 hours. Serve the herrings with the onion and add some soured cream with a little of the marinade poured over the fish.

CHOPPED HERRING

Serves 8

3 large herrings
1 medium-sized apple,
  chopped
3 tbsp onion, finely
  chopped
2 hard-boiled eggs, finely
  chopped

3 slices of white bread,
  crusts removed
1 tsp sugar
1 tsp vegetable oil
3 tbsp wine vinegar
black olives and
  shallots for
  garnishing

Soak the herrings in cold water for about 12 hours. Wash in fresh water, then remove the skin and bones. Finely chop and mix with the apple, onion and eggs. Soak the bread in water for 20 minutes, squeeze out the water, chop the bread and add it to the herrings. Add the sugar, oil and vinegar and mix well. Chill for 3 hours. Garnish with black olives and chopped shallot before serving. Chopped herring was originally a dish made by Russian Jews in Poland. It was very popular and was served as a main course. As time passed, it became a traditional starter for the Sabbath dinner.

HERRING SALAD I

Serves 6

2 large herrings, soaked
  overnight
2 apples, peeled and cubed
2 medium-sized potatoes,
  cooked and cubed
1 large pickled gherkin,
  cubed

1 tbsp onion, finely
  chopped
1 tsp sugar
$\frac{1}{2}$ cup/4 fl oz
  mayonnaise
$\frac{1}{2}$ cup/4 fl oz soured
  cream
4 tbsp wine vinegar
ground black pepper
1 tbsp chopped fresh
  parsley or dill

Soak the herrings in cold water for at least 12 hours. Wash in fresh water, then remove the skin and bones. Cut into pieces about $\frac{5}{8}$ inch long. Mix with the chopped apples, potatoes, gherkin and onion. Add the sugar, mayonnaise, cream, vinegar and pepper, and mix well. Lightly mix in the chopped parsley or dill. Serve on lettuce leaves and garnish with black olives and pieces of tomato.

HERRING SALAD II

Serves 6

2 herrings, soaked
  overnight, skinned,
  boned and cleaned
1 cup/6 oz chopped
  lettuce
2 small onions, thinly
  sliced

2 tomatoes, thinly
  sliced
3 tbsp wine vinegar
3 tbsp vegetable oil
1 tsp sugar
2 green peppers, cubed
$\frac{1}{4}$ tsp black pepper
$\frac{1}{4}$ tsp ground pepper

Cut the herrings into pieces about $\frac{5}{8}$ inch long. Put them in a bowl with the chopped and sliced vegetables. Mix the wine vinegar, oil and seasonings well and pour the dressing into the bowl. Mix well and chill for 1 hour before serving.

Opposite – clockwise from the top: *marinated herring, herring salad II, chopped herring, herring salad I*

GOLDEN SOUP

Serves 8

$3\frac{1}{2}$–$4\frac{1}{2}$ lb chicken
18 cups/7 pints water
2 onions, chopped
2 carrots, chopped
$\frac{1}{4}$ small head of celery, chopped
2 sprigs fresh dill
2 sprigs fresh parsley
salt
freshly ground black pepper
cooked noodles for garnishing

Clean the chicken and boil in the water over a medium flame for 40 minutes. Add the vegetables and herbs and continue cooking the chicken for at least two hours or until the flesh is tender. Remove the chicken and strain the soup. Season to taste. Cut the chicken into small pieces and serve with the soup. Add noodles or a different garnish such as mandeln (see below).

MANDELN

Serves 6 to 8

$1\frac{1}{2}$ tsp all-purpose (plain) flour
1 tsp salt
2 eggs, beaten

Add the flour and salt to the beaten eggs and mix to form a soft dough. Chill for half an hour. Then, with floured hands, form the dough into a roll of about $\frac{1}{4}$ in in diameter and cut into $\frac{3}{4}$ in pieces. Place on a very well-greased baking tray and bake for about 20 minutes at 350°F/Gas 4. Shake occasionally so that they bake evenly. If not serving immediately, reheat in the oven before eating.

KICHLACH

Makes 30 to 40

$\frac{1}{2}$ tsp salt

$\frac{1}{2}$ tsp baking powder

$1\frac{1}{2}$ cups/6 oz all-purpose (plain) flour, sifted

3 eggs

2 tsp sugar

$\frac{1}{4}$ cup/2 fl oz vegetable oil, plus extra for glazing and greasing

1 tbsp sugar and 1 tsp ground cinnamon, mixed for dusting

Preheat the oven to 350°F/Gas 4. Mix the salt and baking powder with the flour. Beat the eggs until frothy and gradually add the sugar, oil and flour while beating constantly. Work the mixture into a light dough and on a floured board roll out to a thickness of about $\frac{3}{4}$ in. Cut into $1\frac{1}{2}$ x 1 in squares. Brush with oil and prick with a fork. Sprinkle on the sugar and cinnamon mixture. Bake on a well-greased baking tray for approximately 20 minutes or until light brown. This recipe is for sweet kichlach. A salted version is traditionally served as a side dish with sliced herrings for the Sabbath dinner.

GEFILTE FISH

There is a rich tradition of fish cooking in Jewish cuisine. According to Talmudic legend, fish is the symbol of fertility and immortality and so should be an integral part of the festive evening meal at *Rosh Hashanah*. The queen among fish on the Jewish menu as well as the pride and joy of each Jewish housewife is gefilte fish, one of the tastiest, most delicious smelling and most beautiful of dishes on every festival table. It is very time-consuming to prepare, but the extraordinary culinary experience makes up for the long hours spent in the kitchen. The procedure described here is certainly not the only method used to prepare this dish. Individual recipes were passed on from generation to generation and each new generation of Jewish housewives improved or perfected in some way the art inherited from their grandmothers. In short, there are as many gefilte fish recipes as there are Jewish households.

Gefilte fish has been an integral part of the festive atmosphere of the Sabbath since time immemorial. A story from the Talmud tells of the Roman Emperor who was a frequent Sabbath guest with the family of a prominent rabbi. He became so enthusiastic about gefilte fish that he asked his cook to make it. Although the Emperor's cook did not depart in the slightest from the instructions which the rabbi's cook had given him, the fish just did not have the same taste and smell as the one at the rabbi's house every Sabbath. The disappointed Emperor asked the rabbi to explain. He told him: "The Jews have special herbs and spices and it is only this that can give the dish the flavour you like so much." The Emperor was very surprised and immediately asked what sort of herbs and spices these were and where he could obtain them. The rabbi replied: "They are very old and we call them 'Sabbath'."

Gefilte fish in portions

GEFILTE FISH

Serves 8 to 10

$4\frac{1}{2}$ lb carp (approximate weight), salt

Clean the fish. Cut into the backbone and remove the spine with the meat; remove the gills, gut the fish, clean and dry thoroughly, and sprinkle with salt on both inside and outside. Fill with the stuffing and sew up using cooking thread. Wrap the fish in a muslin cloth or aluminium foil, place in the boiling sauce and cook very slowly for 45 minutes on each side. Leave the fish to cool in the sauce, then chill in the refrigerator. Carefully remove the wrapping and serve sliced.

For stuffing I
$2\frac{1}{4}$ lb white fish fillet
3 onions, finely chopped
1 tbsp vegetable oil
3 eggs, beaten
1 cup/$3\frac{1}{4}$ oz breadcrumbs or $\frac{3}{4}$ cup/3 oz matzah meal
$\frac{1}{2}$ cup/4 fl oz water
2 tsp salt
1 tsp ground black pepper
1 tsp sugar

Finely chop the fish. Brown the onions in the oil. Remove from the heat and add the eggs, breadcrumbs, water, salt, pepper and sugar to the chopped fish. Mix well and use to stuff the carp.

For stuffing II
Just as stuffing I but add

1 small head of celery or 2 carrots, finely chopped
2–3 slices of stale challah
3 eggs, separated

Add the celery or carrots to the chopped fish and browned onion. Soak the challah in water until soft and then squeeze out the water. Roughly chop the challah and add the egg yolks. Beat the egg whites until stiff and add to the other ingredients, folding in gently.

For stuffing III
$2\frac{1}{4}$ lb white fish fillet, finely chopped

1 onion, finely chopped
2 eggs, beaten
yolk from 1 hard-boiled egg, chopped
1 medium-sized beetroot, grated
2 tbsp grated horseradish
1 tsp salt

Mix all the ingredients together well and use the mixture to stuff the carp.

For the sauce
2 onions, sliced into rings
3 carrots, chopped
2 tsp salt
$\frac{1}{2}$ tsp ground black pepper
1 tsp sugar

Put all the ingredients in a large pan and pour in enough water to cover the gefilte fish. Add the fish, heat gently until the sauce begins to boil.

FISH BALLS

Serves 6 to 8

$3\frac{1}{2}$ lb whole white fish
3 onions, finely chopped
2 tbsp matzah meal
2 eggs, beaten
2 tsp salt
1 tsp ground black pepper
$\frac{1}{2}$ cup/4 fl oz water

For the fish broth

Cleaned fish head, skin
    and backbone
2 carrots, sliced into
    rounds
2 onions, sliced in rings
2 tsp salt
$\frac{3}{4}$ tsp ground black pepper
9 cups/$3\frac{1}{2}$ pints water

Gut the fish, cut off the head, remove the gills, skin and bone, and wash in cold water. Place the cleaned fish head, skin and backbone, along with the other ingredients for the broth, in a large pan and bring to the boil. Leave to simmer while preparing the fish balls. Chop the fish meat very finely and add the onion, matzah meal, eggs, salt, pepper and water. Mix together. With wet hands form the mixture into balls of about 1 in in diameter. Add 3 tablespoons cold water to the simmering broth and then carefully place the fish balls in the liquid. Lower the heat, cover the pan and cook slowly for $1\frac{1}{2}$ hours, removing the lid after 1 hour. Add more seasoning if needed. Leave the fish balls to cool in the broth, then transfer them to individual bowls. Strain the broth and pour over the fish balls. Garnish with the carrot slices. Chill overnight.

PRUNE TZIMMES

Serves 6 to 8

1 medium-sized onion, sliced

1 lb prunes

$3\frac{1}{2}$ lb beef

$1\frac{1}{2}$ tsp salt

$\frac{1}{2}$ tsp ground black pepper

$2\frac{1}{4}$ lb potatoes, peeled and sliced into thick rounds

1 tbsp chicken fat

$\frac{1}{2}$ tbsp all-purpose (plain) flour

juice of 1 lemon

6 tbsp sugar or $\frac{1}{2}$ cup/5 oz honey (clear)

$\frac{1}{2}$ tsp ground cinnamon (optional)

Add the onion and prunes to the beef and pour boiling water over so that the meat is completely covered. Leave to soak overnight in the refrigerator. Add the salt and pepper and cook on a low heat until the meat is tender (approx. 2 hours). Place the potato rounds in a large shallow ovenproof pan and put the meat, onions and prunes on top. Reserve the stock in which the meat was cooked. Preheat the oven to 400°F/Gas 6. Melt the chicken fat in another pan, mix in the flour and, stirring constantly, add 2 cups/16 fl oz of the broth in which the meat was cooked, the lemon juice, sugar or honey and cinnamon (if using). Cook for another 3 minutes, stirring constantly. Pour the sauce over the potatoes and meat and roast for about 40 minutes. Cut the meat into portions before serving.

MEAT KUGEL

Serves 4 to 5

$\frac{1}{2}$ cup/1$\frac{1}{2}$ oz breadcrumbs
    or 2 slices of bread,
    crusts removed
1$\frac{3}{4}$ lb ground beef
1 tsp salt
$\frac{1}{2}$ tsp ground black pepper
1 egg, beaten
1 onion, grated

2 tbsp water or tomato
    juice
2–3 hard-boiled eggs
1 tomato, sliced into
    rounds
1 onion, sliced in rings
2 tbsp chicken fat or
    vegetable oil, plus
    extra for greasing

Preheat the oven to 350°F/Gas 4. If using the slices of bread, rather than the crumbs, leave them in water until soaked through, then squeeze out as much water as possible. Mix together the ground beef, salt, pepper, egg, onion and breadcrumbs or soaked bread. Add the water or tomato juice and mix again. Place half in a well-greased ovenproof dish, smooth the surface and press the eggs into the centre. Cover with the remaining mixture. Decorate the surface with tomatoes and onions, dot over the fat; bake for about 1$\frac{1}{2}$ hours.

VEAL IN PAPRIKA

(Illustrated left)

Serves 4 to 6

3 tbsp vegetable oil
2 onions, finely chopped
2 tsp ground sweet red
    paprika

2$\frac{1}{4}$ lb veal, cubed
1 tsp salt
$\frac{1}{4}$ tsp black pepper
$\frac{3}{4}$ cup/6 fl oz water or
    stock

Heat the oil in a pan, add the onions and fry until lightly browned. Sprinkle with the paprika, add the veal, salt and black pepper. Cover and leave on a medium heat until the meat is tender, adding water or stock occasionally to prevent from drying out.

CHICKEN WITH VEGETABLES AND MUSHROOMS

Serves 4

$3\frac{1}{2}$ lb chicken
salt
freshly ground black
  pepper
2 tbsp vegetable oil
1 medium-sized onion,
  finely chopped
2 green peppers, chopped
$8\frac{1}{2}$ oz mushrooms,
  chopped
1 cup/8 fl oz tomato juice

Cut the chicken into
eight pieces and season
with salt and pepper. Heat
the oil in a large casserole
and add the chicken
pieces. Fry. Add the
onion, peppers,
mushrooms, tomato juice
and enough water to
cover the chicken. Cook
on a low heat for about
30 minutes or until
tender.

GIBLETS WITH MEAT DUMPLINGS

(Illustrated right)

Serves 6

4 tbsp chicken fat
1 onion, finely chopped
$2\frac{1}{4}$ lb poultry giblets
2 tbsp all-purpose (plain)
  flour
4 cups/$1\frac{2}{3}$ pints boiling
  water
$1\frac{1}{2}$ tsp salt
$\frac{1}{4}$ tsp ground black pepper

Meat dumplings
12 oz ground beef
2 tbsp cold water
$1\frac{1}{2}$ tsp salt
$\frac{1}{4}$ tsp ground black
  pepper
2 cloves garlic,
  crushed
1 egg, beaten
1 tbsp matzah meal

Heat the chicken fat in a pan, add the onions and cook
until browned. Add the giblets and fry until browned,
for about 5 minutes. Sprinkle with the flour, add the
salt and pepper and pour the boiling water over. Cover
and cook slowly for 1 hour. Meanwhile mix the ground
beef with the cold water, salt, pepper, garlic, egg and
matzah meal. With dampened hands, form balls the
size of a walnut. Add to the giblet mixture and cook for
a further 20 minutes.

GOOSE WITH CABBAGE

Serves 4 to 5

$3\frac{1}{2}$–$4\frac{1}{2}$ lb goose
3 tsp salt
$\frac{1}{2}$ tsp ground black pepper
4 tbsp goose fat
1 onion, finely chopped
$3\frac{1}{2}$ lb white or red
    cabbage, finely chopped
1 apple, coarsely grated

Preheat the oven to 350°F/Gas 4. Cut the goose into small pieces, season with half the salt and pepper, and roast for approximately 2 hours until tender. Baste it in its juices while it roasts. Heat the goose fat in a large pan and fry the onion until soft. Add the cabbage and stew slowly for approximately 20 minutes. Finally add the apple and the remaining salt and pepper and continue stewing until all the ingredients are cooked. To serve, spread the cabbage mixture out in a bowl and place the portions of roasted goose on top.

GOOSE WITH POTATO STUFFING

Serves 4 to 5

2 cloves garlic, crushed
2 tsp salt
1 tsp ground black pepper
2 tsp ground sweet red
   pepper (paprika)
$3\frac{1}{2}-4\frac{1}{2}$ lb goose

For the stuffing

2 tbsp goose fat
1 onion, finely chopped
goose giblets, finely
   chopped
4 cups/14 oz grated
   raw potato
2 eggs, beaten
2 tsp salt
$\frac{1}{4}$ tsp ground black
   pepper
1 tsp ground sweet red
   pepper (paprika)

Mix together the garlic, salt, black and red pepper. Rub over the skin of the goose and place aside for 1 hour. Meanwhile prepare the stuffing.

Preheat the oven to 350°F/Gas 4. To make the stuffing, heat the goose fat in a pan and add the onion, frying until browned. Add the giblets and fry for 5 minutes. Add the grated potatoes and continue frying for a couple of minutes. Leave to cool, mix in the beaten eggs and add the seasoning. Stuff the goose, sew up or close with steel skewers and place in the oven. Roast for 2–3 hours until the goose is tender. Baste with the juice during roasting.

SCHOLLET

Schollet, or chollent, the traditional Sabbath dish of many generations of Jews living in central and eastern Europe, has not lost any of its fame. It is difficult to imagine a Sabbath dinner without a large pot of warm, delicious-smelling schollet which the housewife takes out of the oven as soon as the whole family returns from the synagogue and sits down at the table.

On Sabbath it is strictly forbidden to make up a fire and so the schollet had to be prepared a day earlier and kept warm until Saturday in a warm oven. This method of preparation was not simple. Housewives simplified their work by sending the raw schollet in its pot to the bakeries where the food was stewed in the great furnaces overnight. After the morning service, the cooked schollet was served by errand boys called *Scholent-jungen*. This joint preparation of schollet was normal in many central European towns and in the Prague Ghetto. In the countryside the pot of schollet was often placed among quilts so the food could be kept warm for a long time.

Philologists still rack their brains over the etymology of the word. The Talmud mentions a dish called *chamin* (from the Hebrew *cham* – warm) and this is what Shephardi Jews call a similar dish. The Ashkenazi word *scholent* (*schalet* or *schollet*) could come from the Old French *chauld* – which also means warm. The French *chauffe-lit*, which means "bed-warmer" could link up with keeping the chollent in quilts. Yet another explanation is that it comes from the German *schul-ende*, meaning "synagogue end", describing the end of the Sabbath service and the time for eating the schollet. A whole number of more or less trustworthy opinions still exist about this name. However, let us now leave the etymological meaning and start with the preparation of schollet, for it tastes wonderful, wherever it comes from!

GOOSE IN SCHOLLET

Serves 6 to 8

2 tbsp goose fat
1 large onion, finely
  chopped
$3\frac{1}{2}$–$4\frac{1}{2}$ lb goose
2 tsp salt
$2\frac{1}{4}$ cups/1 lb yellow peas,
  soaked overnight
$2\frac{1}{4}$ cups /1 lb barley,
  soaked overnight
$\frac{1}{2}$ tsp ground black pepper
$\frac{1}{2}$ tsp ground ginger
4 cloves garlic, crushed
stock or water

Heat the goose fat in a large pan and fry the onion until soft. Clean the goose and cut up into several pieces. Season with the salt and fry with the onions until browned. Add the peas and barley, flavour with the pepper, ginger and garlic and place everything in a large pot. Cover with a little stock or water and stew slowly for approximately 2 hours. Then add more water if it has dried up, cover the pot with a tightfitting lid and leave to cook overnight in a very low oven, 250°F/Gas $\frac{1}{2}$.

POTATO SCHOLLET

Serves 4 to 6

$3\frac{1}{2}$ lb potatoes
2 tbsp vegetable oil
$1\frac{2}{3}$ lb beef
1 tsp salt
$\frac{1}{2}$ tsp ground black pepper
1 onion, finely chopped
3–4 cloves garlic, crushed

Preheat the oven to 250°F/Gas $\frac{1}{2}$. Peel the potatoes and grate finely, then pour away any excess water. Heat the oil in an ovenproof casserole dish. Cube the meat, add the salt and pepper and brown with the onion in the oil. Add the grated potatoes to the meat, mix well, add the garlic, and bake for 30 minutes at 350°F/Gas 4. Cover with a lid and place in the oven overnight at lowest grade.

LAMB SCHOLLET

Serves 4 to 6

$2\frac{1}{4}$ lb lamb, cubed
3 cups/$1\frac{1}{2}$ lb dried haricot
  beans
2 onions, finely chopped
2 tbsp vegetable oil
2 tsp salt
$\frac{1}{2}$ tsp ground black pepper
3 cloves garlic, finely
  chopped

Sort and wash the beans and soak in cold water for about 2 hours. Then cover the beans with fresh water and boil vigorously for 10 minutes. Heat the oil in a large pan. Sprinkle the salt and pepper over the meat and fry together with the onion and garlic. Add the beans and the cooking water and simmer for 2 hours. Add more water to make sure the meat and beans are covered and continue cooking in a very low oven, 250°F/Gas $\frac{1}{2}$ overnight.

SCHOLLET WITH DUMPLINGS

Serves 4 to 6

2 tbsp vegetable oil
$1\frac{1}{4}$ lb beef
2 tsp salt
$\frac{1}{4}$ tsp ground black pepper
1 onion, finely chopped
6 small potatoes
3–4 cloves garlic, crushed
1 cup/7 oz dried haricot
  beans, soaked overnight
$\frac{1}{2}$ cup/4 oz barley, soaked
  overnight

For the dumpling
2 eggs, beaten
2 tbsp vegetable oil
2 tbsp cold water
$\frac{1}{2}$ tbsp salt
$\frac{3}{4}$ cup/3 oz matzah meal

Part cook the beans as in the recipe for lamb schollet. Heat the oil in a large frying pan. Cube the meat, season with salt and pepper and brown in the oil with the onion. Peel the potatoes and, if they are large, cut them in half. Place in a heavy saucepan with the meat. Add the garlic, part-cooked beans and barley. Add enough water to reach about 1½ in above the top of the ingredients. Cook the schollet slowly in the pan or in a warm oven, 350°F/Gas 4, for 3 to 4 hours, adding more water if necessary. In the mean time, make one of the dumpling mixtures. For the plain dumpling, mix together the eggs, oil, water and salt and then add the matzah meal gradually. Work into a firm dough and chill for 20 minutes in the frig. Form into a dumpling or *kishka* and add it to the schollet. Continue cooking at 250°F/Gas ½, overnight.

Meat dumpling

1 cup/3¼ oz breadcrumbs
4 oz ground beef
1 egg, beaten
1 tbsp freshly chopped parsley
3 cloves garlic, crushed
½ tsp grated nutmeg
½ tsp salt
¼ tsp ground black pepper

Mix the breadcrumbs into the ground beef and add the beaten eggs to bind. Add the parsley, garlic, nutmeg, salt and pepper. Form into a dumpling and place in the centre of the schollet to cook as before.

Vegetable kishka

½ small head of celery
2 carrots
1 onion
½ cup/4 fl oz vegetable oil, plus extra for greasing
1¼ tsp salt
¼ tsp ground black pepper
1 tsp ground sweet red pepper (paprika)
1½ cups/6 oz all-purpose (plain) flour, sifted

Preheat the oven to 350°F/Gas 4. Finely grate the celery, carrots and onion; mix thoroughly with the oil. Add the salt, black pepper, sweet red pepper and flour, and mix well. Form into rolls then wrap in a muslin cloth or in aluminium foil greased with oil. Bake the *kishka* for half an hour. Just before the beginning of Sabbath, place the *kishka*, still covered in oil, into the schollet and continue cooking as before. To serve, remove the foil or cloth and cut into portions.

MANDELBROT

Serves 6 to 8

1 cup/8 oz margarine or
   butter, plus extra for
   greasing
$1\frac{1}{2}$ cups/12 oz sugar
4 eggs, beaten
1 tsp vanilla extract
   (essence)
$\frac{1}{2}$ cup /4 fl oz brandy
4 cups/1 lb all-purpose
   (plain) flour, sifted
1 tsp salt
4 tsp baking powder
1 cup/8 oz raisins
1 cup/4 oz dessicated
   coconut
1 cup/4 oz ground
   walnuts
1 cup/$5\frac{1}{2}$ oz blanched
   almonds, finely chopped

Preheat the oven to 350°F/Gas 4. Mix the margarine or butter with the sugar, add
the eggs, vanilla and brandy and continue mixing. Add the flour, salt and baking
powder, mix everything together well and stir in the raisins, coconut, walnuts
and almonds. Bake in a greased dish for approximately 30–40 minutes
until lightly browned.

KUGEL

Our insufficient knowledge of languages leads us to call this festive dish by the name derived from the German "die Kugel" and consider it the feminine form. In fact it has a masculine name, *kugel*, from the Hebrew word *kougal*, meaning round. Originally all kugels were round; nevertheless, in the course of time, Jewish housewives forgot about this and today *kugels* are made in various shapes. The precise definition of the dish is not known. It has many forms and flavours. It can be salty or sweet: there are meat, milk, and potato kugel, or the deliciously sweet *lokschen kugel* made from noodles and fruit.

CHALLAH KUGEL

Serves 4

12 oz challah
2 eggs, beaten
3 apples, peeled and
   thinly sliced
$\frac{1}{3}$ cup/3 oz sugar

4 tbsp vegetable oil,
   plus extra for
   greasing
$\frac{1}{2}$ cup/4 oz raisins
2 tsp ground cinnamon
$\frac{1}{2}$ tsp salt

Preheat the oven to 350°F/Gas 4. Cover the challah with boiling water, leave for a moment, then squeeze out the water and mix in with the other ingredients. Bake in a greased dish for 45–50 minutes until a crust appears on the surface.

PINEAPPLE KUGEL

Serves 4 to 6

6 eggs, beaten
$\frac{1}{2}$ cup/4 oz sugar
4 tbsp melted margarine, plus extra for greasing
$8\frac{1}{2}$ oz crushed pineapple with the juice (you may use canned pineapples)
1 tsp ground cinnamon
1 tsp vanilla extract (essence)
$8\frac{1}{2}$ oz vermicelli or thin noodles
pineapple rings and glacé cherries, to decorate

Mix the eggs with the sugar and add the melted margarine. Add the pineapple, cinnamon and vanilla and stir well. Preheat the oven to 350°F/Gas 4. Boil the vermicelli or noodles in salted water until soft. Drain and mix with the other ingredients. Place the mixture in a well-greased dish and decorate the surface with pineapple rings; place a cherry in the centre. Bake for 40–60 minutes until firm.

LOKSCHEN FRUIT KUGEL

Serves 4 to 6

$\frac{1}{2}$ lb vermicelli or thin
   noodles
2 eggs, separated
2 tbsp vegetable oil, plus
   extra for greasing
2 tbsp sugar
$\frac{1}{2}$ tsp salt
$\frac{1}{2}$ cup/4 oz chopped
   raisins
$\frac{1}{2}$ cup/2 oz grated apple
$\frac{1}{2}$ cup/$\frac{1}{2}$ oz chopped
   walnuts
1 tsp ground cinnamon

Preheat the oven to 350°F/Gas 4. Boil the vermicelli or noodles in salted water until soft. Beat the egg yolks with the oil and add the sugar and salt. Add the drained, hot noodles and mix together. Beat the egg whites until stiff. Add the remaining ingredients and then fold in the egg whites. Bake in a well-greased dish for approximately 45 minutes until golden.

APPLES IN
A PIE CRUST

Makes 15 to 20

$2\frac{1}{2}$ cups/10 oz wholemeal
  flour
4 tsp baking powder
$\frac{2}{3}$ cup/5 oz sugar
1 cup/8 oz margarine
1 egg, beaten
8–10 tbsp milk
15–20 small apples
1 cup/8 oz raisins
beaten egg to glaze
sugar for sprinkling

Mix together the flour, baking powder and sugar, add the margarine and the beaten egg and work into pastry dough using the milk to bind the mixture together. Cover and leave to rest for half an hour. Preheat the oven to 375°F/Gas 5. Roll out the pastry to a thickness of about $\frac{1}{2}$ in. Cut into large squares to fit the size of the apples. Peel and core the apples and fill with the raisins. Place the apples in the centre of the pastry squares, bring the corners together and seal by pressing to form a ball shape. Place the pastry-covered apples on a dry baking tray, brushing the surface of each with beaten egg and bake for about 30 minutes until golden. Sprinkle with sugar before serving.

ROSH HASHANAH AND YOM KIPPUR
ראש השנה יום כפור

Leshana tovah tikatev ve tehatem! "May you be written down and confirmed to have a good year!" These are the words which resound throughout the synagogue after the evening service. It is the first day of Tishri, the beginning of a New Year and also a Day of Judgement. Rosh Hashanah falls at the time when the sign of the zodiac is the "scales" and it is at this time that the Lord lays all our deeds of the past year on the bowls of the scales "to give to every man according to his ways, and according to the fruit of his doings" (Jer. Chap. 17:10). According to Talmudic tradition, at Rosh Hashanah the Lord enters all the righteous people in the Book of Life, and all the wicked in the Book of Death. For all those in between these extremes the judgement remains open till Yom Kippur when the final verdict is decreed. We therefore stand on the threshold of the New Year before God's judgement which shall decide our fate for the whole of the year to come. The two feast days of Rosh Hashanah are the first of 10 days of repentance, also known as *yamim nora'im* (Days of Awe). Unlike the other holidays, a mood of conviviality does not reign during this time. Each person is immersed in his inner self, and searches his conscience and prays for the forgiveness of all his sins. However, repentance does not mean hopelessness; on the contrary, we enter the New Year full of faith in a happy future, because everybody who does penance in time may hope for God's mercy. If a man manages to turn away from sin in time, he will gain forgiveness and shall be entered in the Book of Life for the next year. The present, not the future, decides his fate because "the righteousness of the righteous shall not deliver him in the day of his transgression: for the wickedness of the wicked, he shall not fall thereby in the day that he turneth from his wickedness" (Ezek. Chap. 33:12). So, we must make more of an effort on these days than at any other time, to purge ourselves of evil thoughts and deeds, and live in accordance with God's commandments.

"You sleeper, wake from your sleep, come round from your slumber! Remember your Creator, you who have strayed from the way of truth and walk along the paths of vanity!" The call of the shofar, a ram's horn which can be blown to sound like a musical instrument, concentrates our thoughts during morning and evening services. The shofar was used on many occasions dating back to biblical times. It resounded for the first time when the Lord came down on Mount Sinai to present Moses with the Torah. Here, it is the final urgent summons for repentance as the time of judgement approaches and, also a warning not to disobey its call. At the same time it brings to mind the most significant moments of our past. By listening to the majestic tones of the shofar, we again receive the Lord's kingdom and pledge our obedience to fulfil all His commandments. At the time of repentance and judgement, we appeal in memory of the agreement which we concluded on Mount Sinai to keep the laws, and humbly beg for forgiveness for breaching it so often. The ram's horn also symbolizes the sacrifice of Isaac on the mountain of Moriah. "Abraham lifted up his eyes, and looked, and beheld behind him a ram caught in a thicket by his horns: and Abraham went and took the ram caught and offered him up for a burnt offering in the stead of his son," as is written in the first Book of Moses (Gen. Chap. 22:13). In the tractate of Rosh Hashanah the fate of the ram is compared to the fate of the people of Israel in this world. Just as the ram was caught in a thicket by his horns and thereupon

Left:
Kiddush for the festival of
Rosh Hashanah, Italy, 1470

*Shofars, Bohemia, early
19th century*

sacrified, so shall one misfortune after another befall the people of Israel. They shall wander from exile to exile until they are redeemed and led back to the Promised Land. In the visions of the biblical prophets, the shofar announces the day of the Last Judgement and the coming of the Messiah (Zc. Chap. 9:14). Its trumpet shall resurrect the dead and "they shall come which are ready to perish in the land of Assyria, and the outcasts in the land of Egypt, and shall worship the Lord in the holy mount at Jerusalem" (Is. Chap. 27:13).

On the first day of Rosh Hashanah, after the service in the synagogue, the symbolic ritual takes place of casting out sins in the ceremony of *Tashlich*. It is written: "Thou wilt cast all their sins into the depths of the sea. Thou wilt perform the truth to Jacob, and the mercy to Abraham, which thou hast sworn unto our fathers from the days of old" (Mi. Chap. 7:19–20). We cast out our sins into freshly flowing water full of living fish. Why? Just as a fish is caught in a net, so we are caught in the net of God's judgement and the eye of a fish is always open just like the vigilant eye of God which sees into the most concealed corners of our souls. After reciting the relevant passages from the Books of the Prophets and the Book of Psalms, we shake out all our pockets three times into the water. By this ritual, we symbolically express the hope that like the crumbs from our pockets, so we shall manage to cast away all the sins we have committed in the past year.

When at the festive gathering of Rosh Hashanah the Israelites heard the words of the Torah, they began to weep. However, Ezra and Nehemiah told them: "Mourn not, nor weep… Go your way, eat the fat, and drink the sweet … for the joy of the Lord is your strength" (Ne. Chap. 8:9–10). So today we sit down to the New Year's Day supper with joy and hope in our hearts, and our hope in the good of the coming year is also symbolized by the dishes we shall eat on the evening. The New Year's *challah* looks different from the loaf eaten on the Sabbath and other feast days: it is round so that everything will go well in the New Year and we can enjoy plenty. The loaf is often decorated with ladders and birds made of dough, so that our prayers may climb up to the Lord in heaven. There must be a bowl with honey on the table because this time the *challah* is not dipped in salt, as at other times, but in honey. After consuming a morsel of *challah*, we also dip a slice of apple into the honey and pray for a good and sweet year. The most popular dessert at Rosh Hashanah is honey cakes. *Tzimmes*, a sweet dish made with carrots, is also eaten; in Yiddish carrot is "meren" which also means growth or increase. Tzimmes also symbolizes the desire that next year our priorities and merits should outnumber our faults. We must avoid sinning as much as possible, therefore we must not eat nuts on

נִדְרֵי ׳ וֶאֱסָרֵי ׳ וּשְׁבוּעֵי ׳ וַחֲרָמֵי ׳ וְקוֹנָמֵי ׳ וְקִנּוּסֵי ׳ וְכִ
דְנָדְרְנָא ׳ וּדְאִשְׁתַּבַּעְנָא ׳ וּדְאַחֲרִימְנָא ׳ וּדְאָסַרְנָא
נַפְשָׁתָנָא בִּשְׁבוּעָה מִיּוֹם צוֹם הַכִּפּוּרִים הַזֶה ׳ עַד יוֹ
הַכִּפּוּרִים הַבָּאָה עָלֵינוּ לְטוֹבָה ׳ כֻּלְּהוֹן ׳ דְּאִיחֲרַטְנָא
בְּהוֹן יְהוֹן שָׁרָן ׳ שְׁבִיקִין ׳ שְׁבִיתִין ׳ בְּטֵילִין וּמְבֻטָּ
לָא שְׁרִירִין וְלָא קַיָּמִין ׳ נִדְרָנָא לָא נִדְרֵי ׳ וֶאֱסָרָנָא
אִסָרֵי ׳ וּשְׁבוּעָתָנָא לָא שְׁבוּעוֹת כְּכָת בְּתוֹרַת מ
עַבְדֶּךָ מִפִּי כְבוֹדֶךָ ׳ וְנִסְלַח לְכָל עֲדַת בְּנֵי יִשְׂרָאֵל וְ
הַגֵּר בְּתוֹכָם כִּי לְכָל הָעָם בִּשְׁגָגָה סְלַח נָא לַעֲוֹן הָ
הַזֶּה כְּגֹדֶל חַסְדֶּךָ וְכַאֲשֶׁר נָשָׂאתָה שָׁם בְּמִצְרַיִם וְעַד הֵ
וַיֹּאמֶר יְיָ סָלַחְתִּי כִּדְבָרֶךָ ׳   זֶה ייווי ג פעמים

בָּרוּךְ יוֹתֵה ייָ יֱלֹהֵינוּ מֵה יוֹשׁ קָר בוּ וִ שֶׁהֶחֱיָנוּ וְקִיְּמָנוּ וְהִגִּיעָנוּ לַזְּמַן הַזֶּה
בָּרְכוּ אֶת יְיָ הַמְבֹרָךְ ׳   בָּרוּךְ יְיָ הַמְבֹרָךְ לְעוֹלָם וָעֶד

בָּרוּךְ אַתָּה יְיָ אֱלֹהֵינוּ מֶלֶךְ הָעוֹלָם אֲשֶׁר בִּדְבָרוֹ מַעֲרִיב עֲ
בְּחָכְמָה פּוֹתֵחַ שְׁעָרִים וּבִתְבוּנָה מְשַׁנֶּה עִתִּים וּמַחֲ
אֶת הַזְּמַנִּים וּמְסַדֵּר אֶת הַכּוֹכָבִים בְּמִשְׁמְרוֹתֵיהֶם בָּרָקִיעַ כִּרְצוֹנוֹ בּוֹרֵא
יוֹם וָלַיְלָה גּוֹלֵל אוֹר מִפְּנֵי חֹשֶׁךְ וְחֹשֶׁךְ מִפְּנֵי אוֹר ׳ וּמַעֲבִיר יוֹם וּמֵבִ

Kol Nidre, the Machzor,
Bohemia, c. 1300

New Year's Day. The reason is that the numerical value of the Hebrew letters in the word *egoz* (nuts) is the same as that of the word *chet* (sin).

A week after Rosh Hashanah, we celebrate Yom Kippur, the Day of Atonement. On this day the fate of all of us shall be definitively signed and sealed. We have the last chance to ward off unfavourable judgement. Yom Kippur, the Sabbath of Sabbaths, is a day of rest from all work and is also a day of strict fasting. "And ye shall afflict your souls, and offer an offering made by fire unto the Lord. And ye shall do no work in that same day: for it is a day of atonement, to make an atonement for you before the Lord your

God" (Lev. Chap. 23:27–28), commands the Torah. So our repentance and purging before the Lord is truly deep, we must free ourselves of all bodily needs which could tempt us with sin. So, apart from food and drink, washing, all cosmetics, the wearing of leather shoes, and conjugal relationships are also forbidden. The five forbidden acts correspond symbolically to the five Books of the Torah. On the feast of Yom Kippur no secondary thoughts may divert us from the Torah. On this day we are fully resigned to the will of God. Probably the most emphatic reminder of this fact is the funeral shroud called the *kittel* which the most devout Jews wear. It is a white, loose-cut vestment tied in the middle with a canvas belt. The only decorations allowed are silver buckles. Silver is colourless and white is the colour of purity, repentance and forgiveness.

In order to atone before the Lord, we must first atone before people. So, on the eve of Yom Kippur we seek out those we have offended in any way during the past year and ask them for forgiveness. We make atonement before friends and enemies, settle old scores and pay off debts.

On the 9th of Tishri the evening service begins with the prayer *Kol Nidre* which means "All vows". We pray to the Lord and ask him to forgive us for all the unfulfilled promises we have made in the past year. Before leaving for the synagogue, we sit down to the last meal before the fast. It should be a good square meal but easily digestible so we can endure the long fast well. The meal usually consists of a chicken broth and kreplach filled with finely chopped chicken meat. Kreplach symbolize our hope that the Lord "shall envelop" the strict judgement, which awaits us the next day, with His mercy.

Early the next morning we go to the synanogue. The service lasts the whole day with short intervals. Its main object is the confession of sins – *Vidui* –, the *Avinu malkenu* litany and the prayers of penitence – *selichot*. There is a feeling of solidarity as on all other Jewish feast days: we do not just pray for ourselves but for all the Jews in the world. And we also think of all those close to us who cannot be with us at that moment. When reciting *Yizkor Mazkira* – the prayer for the dead –, the synagogue is always full of people. The climax of the day is the service called *Neila*, closing of the Gates. Then it is nearly nightfall and the gates of heaven are closing. Repentance and prayers of penitence are coming to a close, God's judgements are sealed. The shofar resounds throughout the synagogue for the last time and with the wish for the "next year in the renewed Jerusalem!" everyone returns home.

All week before New Year's Day Shammes Rev's wife and the long-legged Timfeld girl were cleaning up every corner of the prayer house and Shammes Rev got all six children to work and personally made sure that everything was clean and shining. Then the day before the actual feast, he brushed his clothes, smoothed down his ginger-coloured beard and said the words of the prayer. After washing his hands he approached the cupboard containing the Holy Torah scriptures, pulled the string which drew back the red plush curtain and turned the key in the door, behind which stood the sacred scrolls of the Torah. Then, one after the other he carried them to the altar from which tomorrow the cantor would intone, in a tenor voice, that the day had come when everyone had to face the Lord and lay down his scores before the highest judge. One after the other he clothed the scrolls in a white silken and plush cloak with God's name embroidered in gold. On the wooden cylinders, containing the rolled up sacred scrolls of parchment, he placed silver crowns called *rimonim* decorated with bells and sleigh bells, then over them he hung a wrought shining plate with the sign of the Judean lions, secured with a silver chain and a silver pointer *yad* which would indicate the lines to those reading from the Scriptures. When he had finished his work, he walked round the prayer house once more placing a finger on each bench and each candelabrum to make sure there was not a single speck of dust anywhere, and then, with one hand behind his back and the other on his ginger beard, he stopped at each corner looking for cobwebs. Finally he added oil to the eternal light *ner tamid* which hung above the ark of the covenant, changed the red plush curtain to one made of white silk, drew it closed and left the prayer house feeling satisfied. Then he crossed the courtyard and entered a low house with two rooms which stood behind the synagogue in which the Shammes of this *kehila* had always lived with his family.

It was late afternoon, the famous prayer on the eve of the feast would begin in an hour and there were still a few things left to do. Over his clothes he had to place the white funeral shroud called the *kitl*, in which he would be buried one day and in which on that day of judgement he would have to stand before the Lord; then there was the white scarf to get ready which would wrap up the horn or *shofar* by which Fischer the Carter would summon everyone to the highest court of judgement, and he also had to wish his wife *leshono tauvo tikatevu* so she could pray for all that is best and be entered in God's books for the good year because the shammes also has work to do on feast days and does not have time like the others to do this later.

When he had dressed up in his cloak and kissed his wife and children, he returned to the prayer-house and from the cupboard behind the altar which concealed the cups, he took out the boxes for the spices – *besumim* – and other items of worship, and the shofar made of curved ram's horn, wrapped them up in the white scarf which he had brought with him from home and placed them on the altar; then he went to his bench at the wall next to the entrance and placed before him a prayer-book for Rosh Hashanah, and when this ritual ended, he left the bench and went to stand at the door and waited to welcome the first arrivals at the entrance and wish them all the best in their prayers.

Shortly before six, the first people arrived. They came in their festive clothes, suitably dressed and serious, with their wives and older children; in the corridor before the entrance to the prayer-house, they would hug one another and shake hands, and call out to each other:

"Leshono tauvo tikatevu."

"May you be written down and confirmed to have a good year."

And Shammes Rev shook everyone's hand at the door a bit like the host and wished them:

"Leshono tauvo, leshono tauvo, leshono tauvo tikatevu."

Meanwhile Roza prepared the evening meal. They sat down at the laid table and before Roza brought the food, Shammes Rev moved the plate as though by accident and pretended to be surprised when, as every year, he found a letter under it in which his sons thanked their father for everything he had given them in the past year, and promised to be good and hard working in the year to follow. He was moved by this and coughed, but by then Roza was placing on the table the *tzimmes*, the sweet dish of pears, carrot and cabbage with sugar together with a piece of apple soaked in honey accompanied by a wish that the year they were beginning be equally sweet and equally good. However, before they began their meal, Roza would walk round the table and place a piece of fish's head in everyone's mouth so they would be first in everything the following year.

Then when the meal had ended, Shammes Rev would lift up his arms above the table and closing his eyes he would utter words of blessing and then when one son after the other approached him to kiss his hand and wish him good night, it was not the poorest of the *kile*, the church servant, who placed a hand on their heads, but a king whose wealth could not be measured by anyone.

VIKTOR FISCHL, *A Song of Compassion*

Once Rabbi Naftali missed the time when his teacher, the Rabbi from Lublin, used to go to the river for *tashlik*. When the Rabbi returned home with the others, he spotted Naftali running to the river. "Where are you running to?" asked one man from the Rabbi's entourage, "Can't you see that the Rabbi is going home? What good will it do you if you are a little early or late?" – "I want to get there in time to quickly collect the sins which the Rabbi threw into the water," replied Naftali, "and place them in the treasure chest of my heart."

Once, as every year, Rabbi David was spending the New Year in Lublin with his pupil, Rabbi Isaac, at his teacher's, the Seer. Before the trumpeting of the shofar, the Seer looked around him and noticed that Rabbi David was missing. Immediately he sent Isaac to the inn to look for him. Isaac found him

standing before the gate handing a capful of barley to some horses which the driver had not fed because he was in a hurry to get to the prayer-house. When Rabbi David had finished feeding the horses and returned to the prayer-house, the Seer said: "And here Rabbi David has prepared some beautiful trumpeting on the shofar."

On the eve of the Day of Atonement during the distribution of the evening meal which precedes the fast, Rabbi Baruch was handing out sweets to the Hasidim at his table. Meanwhile he was saying: "I love you very much and want to give you anything in the world which I know is good. Observe only what is written in the psalm: 'Savour and see that the Lord is good. Savour rightly and you shall see: where there is something good, there is the Lord.'" And he noted the song: "How good is our God, how pleasant is our lot."

MARTIN BUBER, *Hasidic Tales*

One rich and prominent man from Mikulov did not like Rabbi Shmelke and was constantly trying to put him to shame. On the eve of Yom Kippur he came to him and pleaded with him for reconciliation because it was on this day that everyone forgave one another. He also brought him a jug of very old and strong wine and forced him to drink it as he thought that the *tzaddik*, who was not accustomed to such drink, would get drunk and he would then tell the whole community about it. Rabbi Shmelke drank one glass after another in honour of the Day of Atonement. However when evening drew near and

with it the hour of prayer, a feeling of horror gripped the Rabbi for fear of judgement and he sobered up immediately.

After the evening prayer, Rabbi Shmelke and the other devout men remained in the prayer-house, singing psalms all night as they did every year. When he got to Psalm 41 and the verse "By this I know that thou favourest me, because mine enemy doth not triumph over me", he repeated these words several times and added: "Although there are people who do not like me and try to shame me, forgive them, Lord of the world, so they do not suffer because of me."

MARTIN BUBER, *Hasidic Tales*

MARINATED FISH (GIPIKILTE FISH)

Serves 6 to 8

1 cup/8 fl oz wine vinegar
3 cups of water
1 tbsp salt
4 onions, sliced into rings
4 bay leaves
12 black peppercorns
3 cloves garlic
$\frac{1}{2}$ tsp mustard seeds
$\frac{3}{4}$ tsp chilli powder
$3\frac{1}{2}$ lb carp, cut into
  portions

Mix the vinegar, water, salt, onions and the herbs and spices in a pan and bring to the boil. Add the fish portions and cook on a low heat until tender. Leave the fish in the broth to cool and then strain the liquid into a bowl. Carefully transfer the fish to a deep dish, pour over the strained broth and store covered in the frig. This dish will keep for several days.

BAKED POTATOES FILLED WITH TUNA

Serves 4

4 large potatoes
$\frac{1}{4}$ cup/2 oz chopped green
  pepper
7 oz canned tuna
$\frac{1}{2}$ cup/3 oz mayonnaise
$\frac{1}{4}$ cup/2 oz chopped
  shallot or leek

Preheat the oven to 350°F/Gas 4. Wash the potatoes, prick the skins and bake for an hour, or until they are soft. Cut the baked potatoes lengthways and carefully scoop out the cooked potato. Mix the potato with the remaining ingredients and replace in the scooped out potato skin. Bake for 10 minutes and serve.

FISH SOUP

Serves 4 to 6

Head, bones and tail of a
  large carp (reserving
  the fish for gefilte fish
  or another recipe)
4 tbsp butter
$\frac{1}{2}$ cup/2 oz finely chopped
  celery
$\frac{1}{2}$ cup/2 oz finely chopped
  carrot
1 cup/8 fl oz whipping
  cream
2 tbsp semolina
2 tbsp all-purpose (plain)
  flour
1 egg yolk
salt
ground black pepper
4 slices bread, crusts
  removed
oil for frying

Wash the head, removing the eyes and gills. Place it with the bones into a large
pan containing about $4\frac{1}{2}$ cups/ $\frac{3}{4}$ pint of salted water and bring it to the boil.
Simmer and cook the stock for about $\frac{3}{4}$ hour. Strain the stock into a bowl and
reserve the flesh from the fish head. Heat 1 tablespoon of butter in a pan and fry
the celery and carrot until browned. Add the vegetables to the reserved fish. To
thicken the soup, first whip the cream. Heat another tablespoon of butter and fry
the semolina, add the flour and the remaining butter and mix thoroughly over
medium heat to make a roux. Stir in the whipped cream and finally mix in the
egg yolk. Pour a little of the stock on to this mixture, whisking over low heat to
thicken it. Then add the rest of the stock with the fish and vegetables and
continue cooking over low heat making sure not to boil the soup. Cut the bread
into cubes and fry in oil until golden brown. Serve the soup with the fried bread
cubes.

FARFEL

Another traditional New Year dish is farfel. It is used as garnish for soups or as a side dish with meat. The light and fluffy pieces, made of noodle pastry, symbolize the seed of an abundant harvest in the following year.

FARFEL STEWED WITH MEAT

Serves 4 to 5

1 cup/4 oz wholemeal
  flour
1 cup/5 oz semolina
2 eggs, beaten
2 tbsp poultry fat or
  vegetable oil
$1\frac{1}{4}$ boiled beef or poultry
  meat, cubed
$2\frac{1}{2}$ cups/1 pint stock or
  water
2 tsp salt
$\frac{1}{2}$ tsp ground black pepper

Work the flour, semolina and eggs into a very firm dough. Divide it into three parts and knead each thoroughly. If the dough is not firm enough then add some more flour. Coarsely grate the dough. Leave the grated farfel to dry until the next day. Preheat the oven to 250°F/Gas $\frac{1}{2}$. Leave the farfel to bake slightly in the oven until light brown. Turn up the oven to 300°F/Gas 2. Brown the farfel in chicken fat or oil. Add the meat and cover everything with stock or water. Add salt and pepper and place in the oven. Cover the pot and bake until the farfel is soft and the liquid has been absorbed.

Farfel may also be used as a soup garnish. In this case, instead of baking the dried farfel, boil it in salted water or soup for about 30 minutes.

KREPLACH

A bowl of kreplach, small squares of noodle dough filled with ground meat, is to be found on every festive table. It must be a part of the meal on the four feasts of Simchat Torah, Purim, Shavuot and on the eve of Yom Kippur. The first three feasts are full of joy and happiness, the fourth has a more serious festive atmosphere. It is on this day that the symbolism of kreplach applies: the meat filling personifies the strict justice with which the Lord pronounces over all of us at the final judgement on Yom Kippur, the thin fine pastry on the surface is the symbol of the goodness and mercy which we hope shall cover the strictness of His judgement.

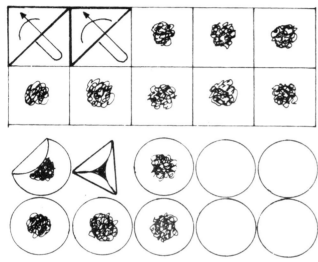

Diagram of the method of making kreplach

KREPLACH

Serves 4

For the pastry
1 cup/4 oz all-purpose (plain) flour, sifted
1 egg, beaten
$\frac{3}{4}$ tsp salt
2 tbsp water
breadcrumbs
oil for frying

For the filling
1 tbsp vegetable oil or poultry fat
1 small onion, finely chopped
1 cup/4 oz ground boiled beef or chicken meat
1 tsp salt
$\frac{1}{2}$ tsp ground black pepper

Work the flour, egg, salt and water into a pastry dough and leave to rest while you prepare the filling. Heat the vegetable oil or poultry fat and fry the onion until browned. Add the meat and fry with the onion for about 5 minutes. Add the salt and pepper and leave to cool. Roll out the dough until it is very thin. Cut into small squares. In the centre place a teaspoon of the filling and fold over the pastry into a triangle. Press the edges firmly together. Boil the kreplach in salted water for approximately 20 minutes or fry on both sides in oil until golden. Serve the boiled kreplach in soup or sprinkled with some fried breadcrumbs.

Kreplach are small unrisen dumplings or triangular dough casings filled with finely minced meat. They are eaten four times a year. Shavuot is one of the important feast days when we eat them. However, at Shavuot, kreplach are not filled with meat or cooked in soup but are filled with cottage cheese and cooked separately. If you have never eaten kreplach you do not know what you are missing.

JIŘÍ LANGER, *Nine Gates*

DUCK WITH APPLE STUFFING

Serves 4 to 6

12 prunes
3 cups/1½ lb cubed apple
1 egg, beaten
4 tbsp breadcrumbs

2 tsp sugar
2 tsp salt
5½–6½ lb duck
¾ tsp ground black pepper
2 cloves garlic, crushed
water or stock for basting

Leave the prunes to soak overnight, then pour hot water over them and carefully stone them. Preheat the oven to 400°F/Gas 6. Mix together the apple, prunes, egg, breadcrumbs and sugar. Stuff the duck with this mixture and sew up. Coat the duck with a mixture of salt, pepper and garlic, and prick the skin lightly with a fork. Roast for approximately half an hour at 400°F/Gas 6, then lower the temperature slightly and roast for 2–3 hours longer until tender. During the roasting remove any excess fat and baste with water or stock.

CHICKEN WITH HONEY AND ORANGE JUICE

(Illustrated left)

Serves 6 to 8

2¼–3½ lb chicken
2 eggs beaten with 2 tsp water
1 cup/4 oz matzah meal
1 tsp salt
½ tsp ground black pepper
vegetable oil for frying

1 cup/8 fl oz water
¼ cup/2 oz clear honey
1 cup/8 fl oz orange juice
¾ tsp ground ginger

Preheat the oven to 350°F/Gas 4. Cut the chicken into pieces and dip into the beaten eggs and water. Coat the chicken in the matzah meal mixed with the salt and pepper. Heat the oil and fry the chicken portions on all sides. Place the chicken in a shallow pan, mix the hot water with the honey and orange juice and pour over the chicken. Sprinkle with ground ginger. Cover and roast for approximately 45 minutes. This dish is delicious with rice.

GOOSE WITH LIVER STUFFING

Serves 4 to 5

$3\frac{1}{2}$–$4\frac{1}{2}$ lb goose
salt

For the stuffing

3 slices white bread,
  crusts removed
oil for frying (optional)
poultry stock or water
2 egg yolks
2 eggs, beaten

2–3 tbsp chicken fat
1 large onion, finely
  chopped
goose liver, chopped
1 tsp salt
$\frac{1}{2}$ tsp ground black pepper
$\frac{1}{2}$ tsp ground ginger
2 cloves garlic,
  crushed
$\frac{1}{2}$ tsp ground caraway
  seeds (optional)

Cube the bread and either dry out in a warm oven or fry in oil. Dampen with stock or water and add the egg yolks and the eggs. Heat the chicken fat and fry the onion until soft. Add the goose liver and cook for 5 minutes. Add the salt, pepper, ginger, crushed garlic and caraway seeds if using, and mix together well. Preheat the oven to 350°F/Gas 4. Coat the goose with salt and fill its stomach cavity or the region under the skin on the breast with the stuffing. Sew up the skin or close with steel skewers. Roast slowly for approximately 2 hours, basting during that time with the juices.

STUFFED BREAST OF VEAL

Serves 8

$4\frac{1}{2}$ lb boned breast of veal
$1\frac{1}{2}$ tsp salt
$\frac{1}{2}$ tsp ground black pepper
1 tsp ground sweet red pepper (paprika)
2 cloves garlic, crushed
3 tbsp vegetable oil
$\frac{1}{2}$ cup/4 fl oz boiling water
stock for basting, as required

For the stuffing

2 cups/$3\frac{1}{2}$ oz coarsely grated raw potato
1 small onion, finely chopped
4 tbsp potato flour
1 egg, beaten
$1\frac{1}{2}$ tsp salt
$\frac{1}{4}$ tsp ground black pepper

To prepare the stuffing, mix together the potatoes, onion, potato flour, egg, salt and pepper. Preheat the oven to 350ºF/Gas 4. Cut open the breast of veal with a sharp knife and fill the cavity with the stuffing. Sew up the meat and coat with the salt, both sorts of pepper and the garlic. Place the breast into a roasting pan with the oil, pour the boiling water over and roast for approximately $1\frac{1}{2}$ hours turning once during this time. During roasting, baste the meat with its own juices, if necessary add a little stock. If any stuffing is left over, make it into a loaf and place in the oven with the meat half an hour before the end of roasting.

LAMB GOULASH

Serves 5 to 6

$3\frac{1}{2}$ lb lamb
2 cloves garlic, crushed
1 tsp ground sweet red
  pepper (paprika)
$\frac{1}{2}$ tsp salt
$\frac{1}{2}$ tsp ground black pepper
4 tbsp all-purpose (plain)
  flour
3 tbsp vegetable oil or
  poultry fat
2 onions, finely chopped
1 cup/5 oz tomato paste
  (purée)
1 cup/8 fl oz boiling water
1 bay leaf
3 potatoes, peeled and
  sliced
1 green pepper, chopped
$1\frac{3}{4}$ cups/$8\frac{1}{2}$ oz frozen
  mixed vegetables

Cut the lamb into large cubes, coat with the garlic, sprinkle with the sweet red pepper, add the salt and pepper and leave to rest for an hour. Dust the cubes of meat with flour. Heat the oil or poultry fat and fry the onion until browned. Add the meat and fry until browned. Add the tomato paste (purée), the boiling water and the bay leaf, cover and cook slowly for 1 to $1\frac{1}{2}$ hours until the meat is almost tender. Then add the potatoes, chopped green pepper and frozen vegetables and continue to cook for approximately 20 to 30 minutes longer.

TZIMMES

This is one of the most popular and also one of the sweetest Jewish dishes. It is so popular that it has entered spoken Yiddish: to do tzimmes with someone means to devote great attention to them, whether they deserve it or not. The name tzimmes is probably derived from the noun *Zimt* which means cinnamon. Tzimmes has countless variations. The most common ingredients are potato, carrot, plum and dried fruit. However, each tzimmes must contain as much sugar or honey as possible. Tzimmes is a welcome dish on every feast, but has a special meaning on Rosh Hashanah when, like *lekach* and other sweet dishes, it personifies our hope for the New Year.

CARROT TZIMMES

Serves 5 to 7

$2\frac{1}{4}$ lb carrots
1 tsp salt
1 tsp sugar
1 tbsp honey
1–2 tbsp butter or
   margarine
$\frac{1}{4}$ tsp ground cinnamon
1 tbsp orange juice

Scrape the carrots, wash and cut into slices. Mix with the salt, sugar, honey and margarine or butter. Add the cinnamon and orange juice and mix well. Cover with water and cook on a low heat for $1\frac{1}{2}$ hours.

APPLE CAKE

Serves 5

6 apples
3 tbsp superfine (caster)
    sugar
$\frac{1}{2}$ tsp ground cinnamon
3 tbsp orange juice
5 tbsp all-purpose (plain)
    flour
1 tsp baking powder
4 tbsp margarine, plus
    extra for greasing
5 tbsp demerara sugar
1 egg, beaten
$\frac{1}{4}$ cup/$1\frac{1}{2}$ oz finely
    chopped walnuts

Preheat the oven to 350°F/Gas 4. Peel and core the apples, cut into rings and add the superfine (caster) sugar, cinnamon and orange juice. Mix together and place in a greased dish. Mix the flour and baking powder in a bowl, add the margarine and work into the mixture until it resembles breadcrumbs. Mix the demerara sugar with the egg and nuts and add to the cake mixture. Place on top of the apples and bake until the apples are tender and the surface is golden.

CARROT CAKE

Serves 8

1½ cups/12 fl oz vegetable oil, plus extra for greasing

2 cups/14 oz sugar

3 cups/6 oz grated raw carrot

4 eggs, beaten

¾ cup/1 oz ground walnuts

3 cups/12 oz all-purpose (plain) flour, sifted, plus extra for dusting

2 tsp baking powder

2 tsp baking soda (bicarbonate of soda)

pinch of salt

2 tsp ground cinnamon

Icing

1 cup/1½ oz cottage cheese

2 tbsp confectioner's (icing) sugar

1 tbsp margarine

1 tbsp lemon juice

Preheat the oven to 350°F/Gas 4. Peel and core the apples, cut into rings and add the superfine (caster) sugar, cinnamon and orange juice. Mix together and place in a greased dish. Mix the flour and baking powder in a bowl, add the margarine and work into the mixture until it resembles breadcrumbs. Mix the demerara sugar with the egg and nuts and add to the cake mixture. Place on top of the apples and bake until the apples are tender and the surface is golden.

TAYGLACH

Makes 30 to 40

For the pastry

3 tbsp vegetable oil, plus
  extra for greasing
1 tsp sugar
$2\frac{1}{2}$ cups/10 oz all-purpose
  (plain) flour, sifted
4 eggs, beaten
pinch of salt
1 tsp baking powder
$\frac{1}{2}$ cup/$2\frac{1}{2}$ oz coarsely
  chopped walnuts

For the syrup

$2\frac{1}{2}$ cup/1 lb clear honey
$\frac{3}{4}$ cup/5 oz demerara
  sugar
4 cups/$1\frac{2}{3}$ pints water
2 tsp ground ginger

Mix the oil, sugar and flour. Gradually beat in the eggs and add the salt and baking powder. Make into a moist and soft dough. Preheat the oven to 350°F/Gas 4. Take a piece of the dough the size of a walnut and, on a floured board, form into a sausage shape about $\frac{1}{2}$ in in diameter.

Press a piece of walnut into the sausage of dough and roll the pastry into a spiral shape. Repeat this process until all the dough has been used up. Place the tayglach on a greased baking tray and bake for about 20 minutes until golden brown. Meanwhile, prepare the syrup. Bring the honey, sugar, water and the ginger slowly to the boil in a large pan. Boil for approximately 15 minutes until the sugar has dissolved completely. Gently add the tayglach to the syrup, a few at a time, cover and cook slowly for 20 minutes. Lower the heat, add the remaining ginger, and move the tayglach around carefully with a slotted spoon so that they don't stick together. Cook for another 10 minutes until the tayglach are golden. (When they are cooked they sound hollow inside when tapped gently.)

Add $1\frac{1}{2}$ cups cold water to the simmering syrup and immediately lift out the tayglach with the slotted spoon. Place on a wet board and leave to cool. Serve at room temperature.

LEKACH

Lekach is the Yiddish for honey cakes, a traditional dish of eastern European Jews. It appears on the festive table for the first time on the first evening of Rosh Hashanah, and is served in great amounts throughout the festival until Yom Kippur. At New Year it is customary to eat sweet dishes which symbolically express our hopes in the "sweet" year to come. However, lekach is not only eaten around New Year. It is a great dessert for every celebration of the joyful events of life, particularly weddings and births.

LEKACH

Serves 8 to 10

1 cup/8 fl oz strong coffee
$1\frac{3}{4}$ cups/8 oz clear honey
3 tbsp Cognac (optional)
4 eggs, beaten
$1\frac{1}{4}$ cup/7 oz demerara
   sugar
4 tbsp vegetable oil, plus
   extra for greasing
$3\frac{1}{2}$ cups/$\frac{2}{3}$ oz all-purpose
   (plain) flour, sifted
3 tsp baking powder
1 tsp baking soda
   (bicarbonate of soda)
1 tsp ground cinnamon
$\frac{1}{4}$ tsp ground cloves
$\frac{1}{4}$ tsp ground nutmeg
$\frac{1}{2}$ tsp ground ginger
$\frac{1}{2}$ cup/$2\frac{1}{2}$ oz chopped
   almonds or walnuts
$\frac{1}{2}$ cup/4 oz raisins

Preheat the oven to 350°F/Gas 4. Mix the coffee with the honey in a pan, bring to the boil, leave to cool and mix with the Cognac, if using. In a large bowl mix the eggs with the sugar and the oil. In another bowl mix the flour, baking powder, baking soda, cinnamon, cloves, nutmeg, ginger, nuts and raisins. Add the flour to the egg mixture, alternating with small amounts of the coffee and honey. Stir in well. Pour the mixture into a greased mould and bake for approximately 1 hour until golden brown.

SUKKOT
שמיני עצרת חג הסוכות
שמחת תורה

The feast of Tabernacles, the harvest festival, a time of joy – these are the names for the feast of Sukkot which begins on the 15th day of Tishri barely a week after the Day of Atonement. By reaching reconciliation with God, other people and ourselves, we get ready to celebrate the most joyous feast of the year. When purified of all sins, we may again fully experience the joy of God's commandments. The time of repentance has passed, the time of joy is here. "Thou shalt observe the feast of tabernacles seven days, after that thou hast gathered in thy corn and thy wine... Seven days shalt thou keep a solemn feast unto the Lord thy God in the place which the Lord shall choose: because the Lord thy God shall bless thee in all thine increase, and in all the works of thine hands, therefore thou shalt surely rejoice" (Deut. Chap. 16:13–15).

In the time of the Jerusalem Temple, Sukkot was the grandest of the three pilgrimage feast. It was celebrated in an atmosphere of carefree joy and thanksgiving for the abundance of the autumn harvest. Thousands of pilgrims throughout the land used to come to the Holy Temple so the Lord could bless the crop of their fields and vineyards. The streets of the city were decorated with colourful garlands of fruit and flowers, wide fans of palm leaves and olive branches. The colours and scents of autumn were everywhere. However, Sukkot was exceptional not only for its splendour and the wealth of the harvest festival. The Torah commands: "Ye shall dwell in booths seven days ... that your generations may know that I made the children of Israel to dwell in booths, when I brought them out of the land of Egypt" (Lev. Chap. 23:42–43). So people left their comfortable dwellings and moved to booths or shelters known as "sukkot" so that they might rejoice there for seven days in the abundance which the Lord bestows on them in the Promised Land, and simultaneously to experience the fate of their ancestors, wandering through the wilderness for 40 years before being able to enter the Promised Land. In rickety makeshift dwellings they were to feel the inconstancy of earthly possessions and become aware that they were left to God's mercy just as their ancestors .

Left:
Mizrach, Slovakia, 18th century

Below:
Erecting a sukkah, Italy,
c. 1470

The biblical celebrations of the feast of Sukkot are just a memory now, but the commandment to live in a sukkah is still observed today. Its construction begins immediately after Yom Kippur, and, because it remains a second home for the full seven days of the feast, people apply great ingenuity and skill to make the sukkah feel like a pleasant and comfortable home. What does it actually look like? This depends very much on the means, ability and imagination of the people who build them. Some are small, humble shelters squeezed on to a balcony or in a tiny yard. Others are luxuriously decorated booths of remarkable size, proudly erected in courtyards and gardens. In spite of the variations, a correctly erected booth must fulfil several conditions. Above all, it must be sufficiently spacious in size to accommodate a table at which the whole family should be able to sit and eat for the entire feast. Three firm walls are needed to withstand gusts of wind. These walls can be made from wooden boards, bricks, stones or metal bars. The most important part of the sukkah is the roof. The roof covering consists of tree boughs, leaves, straw, conifer branches and other natural materials. However, there must be enough gaps to enable a view of the stars. The sukkah should not only be relatively comfortable but also beautiful in appearance, so great attention is paid to the decoration. The walls are hung with red apples, white and black grapes, peppers, eggplants (aubergines), corncobs, and, in warmer regions, dates, figs, oranges, pomegranates. In short, all autumn fruits and vegetables typical of the region are used to express symbolic gratitude to the Lord for all He has endowed us with in this time of the year.

The main commandment for this festival is to live in the sukkah. Each one of God's commandments should be fulfilled with joy and this applies even more strongly during Sukkot, because the Torah specifically says we should be joyful. We enter the sukkah for the first time on the first evening of Sukkot and the first festive meal is taken there. We sit down at the table after sunset when the first three stars appear in the sky.

The grandeur of the harvest festivals of biblical times is reflected in the ingredients of the dishes typical of this feast. All types of autumn fruits and vegetables are used in various combinations – savoury and sweet dishes with fruit or vegetable stuffing, colourful and scented salads, fruit desserts, and lots of fresh fruit and vegetables. However, if bad weather makes it impossible to enjoy fulfilling the commandment, it is enough to say all the obligatory blessings, take a sip of wine and eat a little bread in the sukkah. The evening meal can then be eaten in the warmth of the house. If the weather allows, then at least two main meals are eaten in the sukkah for the seven

Kiddush in a sukkah, Italy, 15th century

Table in a sukkah with lulav and etrog

days of the feast; devout Jews also sleep there. Apart from these two activities, the sukkah, as a house of God, is suitable for the study of the Torah, devout meditation and discussion of the commandments. It is here that the unique atmosphere of these feasts can be experienced to the full, and because a joy shared is a joy doubled, this temporary dwelling is open to everyone who wishes to enter and spend time with us. Visitors to the sukkah are not only the usual guests of flesh and blood; it is at Sukkot that the seven holy guests or *ushpizin* – the forefathers Abraham, Isaac, Jacob and Moses, Aaron, Joseph and David – spend time beneath our roofs. Each evening one of them comes down from the Garden of Eden to share our time of joy. So, after entering the sukkah, we say a word of welcome and sometimes hang up a plaque on the sukkah wall with the text.

"And ye shall take you on the first day the boughs of goodly trees, branches of palm trees, and the boughs of thick trees, and willows of the brook; and ye shall rejoice before the Lord your God seven days" (Lev. Chap. 23:40). This commandment – to take the four species of tree, *arba'a minim* – is the main ritual on the feast of Sukkot. The most important is the *etrog*, a citrus fruit from a cultivated tree resembling the lemon. Time and care should be taken in selecting it: it should be fresh, a beautiful colour, regular in shape and without any blemishes.

The following story shows how dear this commandment is to us: a poor *tzaddik* (pious Jew) saw a wonderful etrog in a market on the eve of Sukkot and very much wanted to have it. However, he did not earn enough money to buy it so decided to sell the precious *tefilin* (phylacteries) he had inherited from his forefathers to buy the *etrog*. When he came home and boasted to his wife about what he had done, she got very angry and flung the *etrog* on the floor so it could no longer be used. The tzaddik then said: "I sold the *tefilin*, lost the *etrog*, am I to fall into the pit of rage?"

The branches of date palms are called *lulav* in Hebrew, a myrtle twig is *hadas* and the twig of a brook willow is *arava*. The Talmudic tractate *Sukkah* specifies the criteria according to which these branches and twigs should be selected and also

Etrog vessel, 18th century

states their precise number: one palm bough, two willow branches and three myrtle twigs are required to fulfil the *mitzvah* (commandment). At the end of the Sukkot morning service, for the whole of the festival except the Sabbath, the *etrog* is held in the left hand, the *lulav*, *hadas* and *arava* tied together into one bunch in the right, and a special blessing is said. During part of the service called Hallel, this bunch is waved in different directions and then up and down. This is to symbolize all the corners of the world and God's rule over the entire earth. Each of the four species of tree symbolizes the good and less good qualities of God's people (*Midrash Vayikra Raba* 30). The best *etrog*, endowed with a delicious taste and a pleasant scent, represents the people of Israel who study the Torah and also carry out good deeds. Dates have a wonderful taste, but they have no smell and so the *lulav* personifies those who fervently study the Torah although their studies are not accompanied by the carrying out of good deeds. The opposite is true of the myrtle: it has a lovely scent, but cannot be eaten, and it signifies those who carry out good deeds but neglect the study of the Torah. The willow has neither taste nor scent, like the lives of those who do not study the Torah and do not carry out good deeds. All these people are joined together in one firm and inseparable group, just like the *etrog, lulav, hadas* and *arava*. They

have to rely on each other and complement one another. The sinners sin and the devout and just repent on their behalf and purify them with their good deeds. According to a different interpretation (*Midrash Agada*), the four species of tree correspond to the individual parts of our body: *etrog* is the heart, the slim and erect *lulav* is the spine, *hadas* the eye and *arava* the mouth.

After *musaf* (the additional prayer), a ritual called *hoshanot* is carried out on each day of the festival during which the rabbi, cantor and the congregation of worshippers carry the four species and walk once around the synagogue. During this procession a prayer for salvation and the renewal of the Temple is said. *Hoshana* means "have mercy", "help us!", and provides the derivation for the name of the ritual. The feast culminates on the seventh day, *Hoshana raba*. On this day the worshippers go round the bimah seven times while the bunches of willow branches are struck against the floor; their falling leaves symbolize the falling sins, the rain falling from heaven and the eternal life cycle in nature based on constant disappearance and renewal. This day is often considered to be a sort of epilogue – the Day of Reconciliation, the last chance to avert the unfavourable judgement of heaven by repenting. That is why the same dishes are eaten as during the High Feasts: round *challah*, honey cakes, sweet dishes and kreplach filled with meat. Sukkot ends on this day but we do not return to an ordinary week day. There are still two feast days awaiting us which follow on straight after Sukkot. "On the eighth day ye shall have a solemn assembly: ye shall do no servile work therein", (Num. Chap. 29:35). The eighth day of the feast of Sukkot was a day of festive gathering and rest. Since the freedom from Babylonian rule and the dedication of the first temple, it has been celebrated on the 22nd of Tishri as the separate feast of Shemini Atzeret – the "eighth (day) of solemn assembly". According to tradition, the Lord carried out judgement over all the waters of the world and therefore we ask him to send us enough rain for the entire year and protect us from floods. We express this wish in the prayer *Tefilat geshem* which is the main part of *musaf* on this festival.

In the countries of the Diaspora, the day after *Shemini Atzeret* (the 23rd of Tishri) is called Simchat Torah – Rejoicing of the Law. However, in Israel these two days of the festival are combined. The weekly readings of the Pentateuch which have taken a whole year come to an end and then begin again from the first verse of Genesis. One cycle is completed and a new one begins; the regular repetitive cycle never stop and so is like the way rain alternates with drought in nature. Each end means a new beginning, rejoicing of the Torah is eternal and undiminishing. All the scrolls of the Torah are taken out of the Ark and the worshippers carry them round the synagogue seven times. The adults are followed by jubilant children jumping about and waving paper flags. Everyone is happy, singing and dancing to traditional and modern Hebrew and Yiddish songs. The last festival reading of the law is called *sidrah*. On this occasion, unlike other festivals, all the men over 13 – *barmitzvah* age – are called up to the reading. So the last part of the five books of Moses is read and immediately the synagogue is filled with the first words of God's Torah: "In the beginning God created the heaven and the earth."

Above and right:
Povijan for the Torah (detail),
Moravia, 18th century

In my yard stands the *sukkah* – the booth I have built for the holiday, covered with branches, and around me the forest looks like a huge *sukkah* designed for God Himself. Here, I think, God celebrates His *Sukkot*, here and not in town, in the noise and tumult where people run this way and that panting for breath as they chase after a small crust of bread.

As I said, it is the evening of *Hoshana raba*. The sky is a deep blue and myriads of stars twinkle and shine and blink.

"Be quiet, Golde," I tell her, "have you forgotten that today is the seventh day of the feasts of "Under Green?" It is on this night that our fates are decided and the verdict is confirmed. We have to stay up this night. Listen to me, Golde, be so good as to put the samovar on the boil and make some tea, while I go and hitch up the horses. I'll ride to the station with Hodl."

SHOLOM ALEICHEM, *Hodl*

That year *etrogs* were very rare and they did not get one in Korec. On the first of the festival the entire village waited in prayer in case someone would bring some from one of the neighbouring towns which promised them help. But the morning prayer ended and no one appeared. So they ordered the prayer leader to begin with the festive liturgy. Hardly had he uttered the blessing when a black *melamed* emerged from behind a rock, came forward and said, "Do not start yet." The

people did not notice anything until the prayer leader, whom they asked why he was hesitating, referred them to Rabbi Pinchas and took him to ask. "The *etrog* shall appear at the right time," he told them. An hour had not gone by when a farmer on horseback arrived at the prayer-house and stated that he was bringing something for Rabbi Pinchas. It was an *etrog* and a letter. Rabbi Pinchas took the *etrog*, asked for a bunch of palm branches and uttered a blessing.

MARTIN BUBER, *Hasidic Tales*

After the destruction of the second Temple, it became a custom in Jerusalem during Sukkot to climb the Mount of Olives opposite the Temple and pray there. On *Hoshana raba*, the seventh day of the feast of Sukkot, it was a custom to walk round the Mount seven times and look in the direction of the Temple. Jews flocked in to celebrate the festival from the surrounding lands and even from overseas. Of course, they had to be accommodated and therefore it was decided to erect many tabernacles (sukkot) in the courtyards of synagogues and on the roofs of houses although everyone erected his own sukkah in which he could eat, drink, study the Torah and sleep.

An important tradition in Jerusalem was also the laying of a scarf before the entrance of the tabernacle. This scarf was to remind passers-by that they were welcome to enter and could take part in a festive meal. The removal of the scarf was a sign that the food had been eaten and that people should no longer enter. Nevertheless, visitors do enter the sukkah whether or not the scarf is laid out, because among the visitors to the tabernacle there are seven *ushpizin* or guests who see "but are not seen" – the beloved Abraham, the holy priest Aaron, the just Joseph and the messianic king David.

Each day one of them takes the place at the head of the holy party which visits the tabernacle.

PHILIP GOODMAN, *Sukkot and Simchat Torah*

We would observe feast days with pomp. Of course we the children liked "under the green" festival of Sukkot (of Tabernacles) best.

In memory of the fact that our ancestors lived in tents in the wilderness for forty years, we the descendants also eat in a tent or booth (sukkah) for eight days. This sukkah was built onto the house. It had a beautiful wooden lattice ceiling for a roof with a cover above it. We would erect and decorate our tent a whole week before the festival, making stars out of silver paper and coloured paper drains, tied with gilt-covered

nuts. Then I would walk around and pick flowers for the basket, as far as the pheasant run and the Hornbeam at the foresters' for brushwood and everything was ready on the eve of the festival. The brushwood was placed on the lattice roof, the covers were opened and everything glistened inside. After synagogue we would all sit down inside the tent, Mother brought a very big and hot evening meal as food in an open place without a roof got cold very quickly, and we would eat with grandeur. It was happy when Father would praise my week's work.

SIMON WELS, *At Bernat's*

Farmers bring deciduous twigs and brushwood from the forests as they know only too well when the Jews want to enjoy themselves. Their arrival is followed by arguments, haggling and crowding around this beauty of the forest. I particularly like the children! With twigs on their heads and under their arms, the boys and girls tear down the streets. The old high houses appear to smile and look younger. Then the stalls are set up. The children bring treasures that they have prepared long in advance: gilt apples, nuts and paper strips to decorate the walls. It is at this time that itinerant tradesmen receive the

best returns for their pictures. The smallest of the children spend their very last pennies to acquire several of the coloured scrawled pictures.

Now the leaves are laid down through which peep and sparkle golden stars, long colourful paper lanterns. Then the mother or father comes to examine the children's work, the proud sparkling spectacle on the twigs and walls. Now and then even the father takes hold of an axe or tightens up a screw.

Also a part of the feast "under the greenery" are palm leaves *lulav* and *etrog* (ritual plants used for Sukkot). Asia and the Ionian islands are the homeland of the *etrog* which smells as sweet as Solomon's Song of Songs. Great care is devoted to such an *etrog*. It must bear no blemish otherwise it would be a sin to use it. Affluent people show it off. They have a silver box in which the precious fruit rests on soft flax. During the service in the synagogue the *lulav* with the *etrog* is raised and lowered in a mystical motion. The leaves strike against each other and it seems as though we are in the middle of a forest.

LEOPOLD KOMPERT, *Randar's Children*

The feast of Simchat Torah fell on a Friday. Ezriel went from one Kiddush to another. He drank dry wine, sweet wine, mead with nuts and beer with the celebrants. He ate strudel, cakes, gâteaux. Cipele offered him cabbage with raisins and herbal sauce. He had overeaten and was in high spirits.

Yes, for the Hasidim the day was a feast of joy of the Torah. It grew dark. With the sunset the women hurried with the blessing over the candles. Kaile, Cipele's girl, prepared the food for Shabbat and filled the oven with dough. She would soon break into the song *"Lecha dodi..."*, and the mood of Shabbat would fall upon her. Then they would again begin to recite the first paragraph of Genesis.

In the evening they went to the prayer-house again. The candles and paraffin lamps still burned. The floor had been swept and covered with yellow sand. The Hasidim recited the Song of Songs. The cantor stood at the stand and began with "Come close and let us rejoice of the Lord...".

ISAAC BASHEVIS SINGER, *Simchat Torah*

Rabbi Isaac Baer was very poor in his youth. One year he had to fast after as well as before the Day of Atonement, and when the Feast of Tabernacles drew near he did not have the wherewithal to celebrate it. So he stayed in the House of Study after prayer, for he knew that there was no food in his house. But his wife had sold a piece of jewelry she still had, without telling him about it, and had bought holiday loaves and potatoes and candles for the sum she received.

Toward evening when the rabbi came home and entered the Sukkah, he found a festive table awaiting him, and was filled with joy. He washed his hands, seated himself, and began to eat the potatoes with great gusto, for he had gone hungry for days.

But when Rabbi Isaac Baer grew aware of how preoccupied he was with eating, he stopped. "Berell," he said to himself, "you are not sitting in the sukkah; why, you are sitting right in the bowl!" And he did not take another bite.

MARTIN BUBER, *Hasidic Tales*

A pair of lions,
South Bohemian tabernacle, 1820

EGGPLANT (AUBERGINE) SALAD WITH MAYONNAISE

Serves 3

1 medium-sized eggplant
  (aubergine)
3 tbsp vegetable oil
1–2 cloves garlic, finely
  chopped
$\frac{1}{2}$ large onion, sliced in
  rings
3 tbsp mayonnaise
juice of half a lemon
salt
ground black pepper

Peel the eggplant, cut in half and cube. Heat the oil in a pan. Sprinkle the eggplant with salt and fry until golden. Leave to cool and then mix the eggplant in a bowl with the garlic, onion rings, mayonnaise, lemon juice, salt and pepper. Chill overnight. Serve with toasted bread.

MARINATED EGGPLANT (AUBERGINE) SALAD

Serves 4 to 6

3 sweet peppers
1 medium-sized eggplant
  (aubergine)
oil for frying
$1\frac{3}{4}$ lb tomatoes, peeled
  and sliced
1 onion, sliced into rings
1 large clove garlic, finely
  chopped
5 tbsp wine vinegar
salt
ground black pepper

Chop the peppers into large pieces, cut the eggplant into quarters and then cut across into thin slices. Heat the oil in a pan, fry the peppers and eggplant quickly, and drain on kitchen paper. In a large bowl mix the peppers, eggplant, the tomatoes, onion, garlic, vinegar, salt and pepper and mix well. Cover the bowl and leave to marinate in a refrigerator for at least 2 days.

Right:
*Above: marinated eggplant
(aubergine) salad;
below: eggplant (aubergine)
salad with mayonnaise*

EGGPLANT (AUBERGINE) "OLIVES"

Serves 4

2 medium-sized
   eggplants (aubergines)
3 eggs, beaten
oil for frying
1 small onion, finely
   chopped
2 tbsp freshly chopped
   parsley
$1\frac{3}{4}$ lb ground beef
1 tsp salt
1 tsp ground black pepper
3 tbsp long-grain rice
$\frac{1}{2}$ tsp sugar
$\frac{1}{4}$ cup/2 fl oz water
1 cup/8 fl oz tomato juice
1 tbsp chicken fat or
   parve margarine

Peel the eggplant and cut lengthways into $\frac{1}{2}$ in slices. Coat in half the beaten eggs, heat the oil in a pan and then fry the slices on both sides until browned. Remove from the oil and put aside. Next brown the onion and parsley in the same oil. Mix the remainder of the eggs into the meat, and add the salt, pepper and rice. Add this mixture to the onion in the pan and fry until the meat turns brown. Preheat the oven to 350°F/Gas 4. Take a teaspoon of the mixture and place it on an eggplant slice, then roll it up. Place the rolls in a baking dish, sprinkle with the sugar, add the water, tomato juice and chicken fat or margarine. Bake for approximately 35 minutes.

EGGPLANT (AUBERGINE) BAKED WITH CHEESE

Serves 4

1 large eggplant (aubergine)

vegetable oil for frying, plus extra for greasing and drizzling

4 eggs, beaten

1 cup/2 oz grated Parmesan, Cheddar or other strong cheese

1 cup/4 oz boiled rice or boiled and mashed potatoes

1 tbsp freshly chopped parsley

1 tbsp chopped fresh rosemary or 1 tsp dried rosemary

1 tbsp chopped fresh basil

2 large tomatoes, peeled and sliced

1 tsp salt

Preheat the oven to 300°F/Gas 2. Cut the eggplant into $\frac{1}{4}$ in slices. Heat the oil in a pan and brown the eggplant slices on both sides. Place half the slices on the bottom of a well-greased ovenproof dish. Mix together the eggs, cheese and rice or potatoes and use this mixture to cover the eggplant slices. Cover the surface with the remaining slices, sprinkle with the herbs and tomatoes. Sprinkle with salt and drizzle on a little oil. Bake for 45 minutes to 1 hour until a crust forms on the surface.

BEEF GOULASH

Serves 10

2 tbsp vegetable oil
2 onions, thinly sliced
$2\frac{1}{4}$ lb beef, cubed
1 tsp salt
$\frac{1}{4}$ tsp ground black pepper
2 tsp ground sweet red
   pepper (paprika)
1 green pepper, chopped
1–2 tomatoes, peeled

Heat the oil in a large pan. Brown the onion, add the meat and fry on all sides. Add the salt, black pepper and sweet red pepper, cover and simmer for 2 hours. When the meat is almost tender, add the green pepper and the tomatoes and continue to cook until the meat is tender. Bread dumplings, which are particularly popular in Bohemia, can be served as a side dish.

Bread dumplings

3 cups/12 oz
   wholemeal flour
$1\frac{1}{2}$ tsp salt
3 tsp baking powder
1 egg, beaten
1 egg yolk
$2\frac{1}{2}$ cups/1 pint soda
   water
7 bread rolls, cubed

Mix the flour with the salt and baking powder in a large bowl. Add the whole egg, the extra yolk and the soda water, and work into a soft dough. Knead for approximately 15 minutes. Leave the dough to rest for 15 minutes and then gradually mix in the pieces of bread roll. The dough should be heavy so add more roll as necessary to achieve the correct consistency. On a floured board divide the dough into five pieces and form a long sausage shaped dumpling approximately $2\frac{3}{4}$ in in diameter from each piece. Boil the dumplings in a large pan of boiling water for 15 to 20 minutes, and then drain. Cut the lengths of dumplings into pieces while they are still hot.

BEEF WITH SAUERKRAUT

Serves 5 to 7

2 tbsp vegetable oil
2 onions, finely chopped
$2\frac{1}{4}$ lb prime beef, cubed
1 tsp salt
$\frac{1}{4}$ tsp ground sweet red
  pepper (paprika)
$1\frac{1}{4}$ lb sauerkraut
1 bay leaf
1 cup/8 fl oz boiling
  water
$8\frac{1}{2}$ oz smoked poultry
  or beef salami, cubed

Heat the oil in a large pan, add the onions and fry until browned. Add the cubed meat and fry on all sides. Add the salt and sweet red pepper. Cover and stew gently for about half an hour. Chop the sauerkraut and add to the meat. Continue cooking for about 10 minutes. Add the bay leaf, pour in the boiling water and cook until the meat is tender, about $1\frac{1}{2}$ hours. Remove the bay leaf, add the smoked poultry or salami and continue cooking for a few more minutes.

STUFFED VEGETABLES

Serves 4

8 sweet peppers
10 medium-sized
　potatoes or 3 small
　zucchini (courgettes)

For the stuffing

$1\frac{1}{4}$ lb ground beef or lamb
1 small onion, finely
　chopped or grated
2 tbsp freshly chopped
　parsley
1 tsp salt
$\frac{1}{2}$ tsp ground cinnamon
$\frac{1}{4}$ tsp ground nutmeg
$\frac{3}{4}$ tsp ground black pepper
1 egg, beaten
$\frac{1}{2}$ cup/2 oz matzah meal

For the sauce

$1\frac{1}{4}$ lb tomatoes, peeled
　and sliced
1 cup/8 fl oz tomato
　juice
$\frac{1}{2}$ cup/4 fl oz water
2–3 garlic cloves,
　crushed
$\frac{3}{4}$ tsp ground black
　pepper
pinch of cayenne
　pepper

Cut the vegetables lengthways, remove the seeds from the peppers, cut off the zucchini stalks and scoop out the flesh leaving an outer layer of about $\frac{5}{8}$ inch. Peel the potatoes, cut in half and scoop out the insides. To make the stuffing, mix all the ingredients together in a bowl and add the matzah meal gradually to prevent the mixture from being too runny. Fill the prepared vegetables up to the brim with the stuffing. To make the sauce, place the tomatoes, tomato juice and water in a pan, add the remaining sauce ingredients and carefully place the stuffed vegetables on top. Bring the sauce to the boil, cover the pan and cook gently for 30–40 minutes. They can also be baked in the oven at 300°F/Gas 2 for 40 minutes.

POTATO DUMPLINGS

Serves 6

4 cups/7 oz potatoes,
  boiled and grated
3 tsp salt
1 cup/5 oz semolina
$\frac{1}{2}$ cup/2 oz potato flour
1 cup/5 oz wholemeal
  flour
1 egg, beaten

Mix the potatoes with the salt, semolina, potato and wholemeal flour and the egg. Work into a dough and form into a sausage shape approximately 2 in in diameter. Cut into 4 pieces and form 4 elongated dumplings rounded off at the ends. Bring a large pan of water to the boil, add the dumplings and cover. Turn the dumplings over while cooking. After 15 minutes check to see if they are cooked inside and, if so, take out carefully. If not cooked through, return to the water and cook for not more than 5 minutes. It is best to cut up the dumplings and either boil them to reheat or fry in fat before serving. They may be roasted, sprinkled with onion browned in fat. Serve as a side dish with meat or vegetables.

HOLISHKES

One cannot imagine Sukkot without holishkes: the stuffed cabbage leaves which are a traditional dish of eastern European Jews. This type of dish is known in various forms and has several different names. In Russia they are called "galuptze", in Romania "sarmali" and in Armenia "dolmas". The tradition of this dish dates back to biblical times when vine rather than cabbage leaves from the sunny slopes of Palestine were used.

HOLISHKES

Serves 6

1 large cabbage

For the stuffing
$1\frac{2}{3}$ lb ground beef
2 cloves garlic, crushed
2 eggs, beaten
4 tbsp raw long-grain rice
1 tsp salt
$\frac{1}{2}$ tsp ground black pepper
1 medium-sized onion, grated
3 tbsp cold water

For the sauce
$1\frac{2}{3}$ lb tomatoes, peeled and sliced
2 cups/1 pint tomato juice
1 clove garlic, finely chopped
1 tbsp demerara sugar
salt
ground black pepper

Cut the stalk out of the cabbage. Bring a large pan of water to the boil and blanch the cabbage. Separate the cabbage into individual leaves and allow to drain. The cabbage can be stored like this in a freezer for 2 days and defrosted before cooking. The leaves will be soft and do not have to be cooked.

To prepare the stuffing

Mix the meat with the garlic, egg, rice, salt, pepper, onion and water. Place 1 tablespoon of meat filling on each cabbage leaf and roll up. Preheat the oven to 300°F/Gas 2. Put the stuffed leaves in an ovenproof dish, pour the sauce over, cover and bake for approximately $1\frac{1}{2}$ hours. Then uncover and bake for half an hour longer.

To prepare the sauce

Mix together the tomatoes, tomato juice, garlic and demerara sugar and season to taste. Bring the mixture to the boil and then simmer gently for approximately 15 minutes.

An alternative method

Omit the garlic in the stuffing and the sauce and add $\frac{1}{4}$ cup/2 oz raisins instead. After cooking for $1\frac{1}{4}$ hours add 3 tablespoons of honey and $\frac{1}{4}$ cup/$2\frac{1}{2}$ fl oz lemon juice to the sauce and continue to cook for another half-hour.

POTATO LOAVES

Serves 5 to 6

$1\frac{1}{4}$ lb potatoes
1 tsp salt
$1\frac{3}{4}$ cups/7 oz wholemeal flour
2 tbsp potato flour
1 egg, beaten, 1 egg yolk
2 tbsp chicken or goose fat
1 bread roll

Boil the potatoes in their skins for about half an hour or until they are cooked. Allow to cool, and then peel. Chop finely on a floured board, sprinkle with the salt and add the flour, potato flour, egg and egg yolk. Knead the dough. Divide into two halves and roll each half into a cylinder approximately 2 inches in diameter. Cut these downwards into 1 inch pieces, rounding them off to form "loaves". Place into boiling salted water and cook for 4–5 minutes. Remove from the water using a slotted spoon or ladle and leave to drain. Heat the poultry fat in a pan. Grate the bread roll and fry the breadcrumbs until golden, roll the potato shapes in the breadcrumbs, shake lightly and leave for a minute in a warm oven. Serve as a side dish.

POTATO ROLL

Serves 8 to 10

10 medium-sized
    potatoes
$1\frac{1}{2}$–2 cups/6–8 oz
    wholemeal flour
$\frac{1}{2}$ cup/3 oz semolina
2 tbsp potato flour
1 tbsp salt
1 egg, beaten

For the filling

12 oz ground poultry
    salami or cooked and
    ground smoked beef.

Stewed sauerkraut

Serves 8 to 10

$2\frac{1}{4}$ lb sauerkraut,
    chopped
pinch of salt
$1\frac{1}{2}$ tsp caraway seeds
1 potato, peeled and
    grated

Boil the potatoes, allow them to cool slightly and then peel and grate or chop finely. Work the potatoes, flour, semolina, potato flour, salt and egg into a dough on a board. Roll out to a thickness of about $\frac{5}{8}$ in. (If the dough is sticky, sprinkle with flour.) Spread the meat filling on one half of the dough and roll up. Press down the edges firmly to seal. Wrap the roll in a wet teacloth and carefully transfer to a roasting pan. Add enough boiling water to come halfway up the sides of the roll. Cover the pan (probably using another pan will be easiest) and cook over moderate heat for 25 minutes. Then turn over the roll and cook for a further 20 minutes. Transfer the cooked roll carefully to a board. Allow the steam to escape and then remove the teacloth. Serve with stewed sauerkraut. It is delicious fried in oil the next day.

Stew sauerkraut in a small amount of water, and add salt and the caraway seeds. When half stewed, add the potato and the apple and stew until tender.

FLUDEN
(Illustrated right)

Serves 10 to 12

$\frac{1}{2}$ cup/4 oz sugar, plus
1 tsp and a little extra
    for sprinkling
$\frac{1}{4}$ cup/$2\frac{1}{2}$ fl oz milk
$\frac{1}{2}$ oz fresh yeast
4 cups/1 lb all-purpose
    (plain) flour, sifted
2 cups/1 lb margarine
    or butter, plus extra
    for greasing
4 eggs, beaten
8 tbsp sweet wine
$\frac{1}{4}$ tsp salt
beaten egg for glazing
1–$1\frac{1}{2}$ cups/6–8 oz plum
    jelly (jam)

Stir 1 teaspoon of sugar into the milk and heat very gently until lukewarm. Crumble the yeast into the milk and

→

leave to stand in a warm place for a couple of minutes. Add the flour, margarine or butter, sugar, egg, wine and salt, and work into a smooth pastry. Leave to rest for an hour. Meanwhile prepare the filling.

For the apple filling
4–5 grated apples
1 tsp ground cinnamon
$\frac{1}{2}$ cup sugar or 2 tbsp honey

Mix the apples with the cinnamon and sugar or honey.

For the poppy-seed filling
$\frac{1}{4}$ cup/2 fl oz water
3 tbsp sugar

$8\frac{1}{2}$ oz ground poppy seed
1 egg white
juice of half a lemon
juice of half an orange
$\frac{1}{2}$ tsp ground cinnamon
1 cup/8 oz raisins
1 tbsp rum
$\frac{1}{4}$ cup/2 oz margarine

Heat the water in a bainmarie. Add the sugar and stir until dissolved. Add the poppy seed, egg white, lemon and orange juice, cinnamon, raisins and rum and heat for 5 minutes, stirring constantly. Add the margarine and continue cooking for a few more minutes until it melts. Leave to cool.

For the nut filling
1 cup/4 oz ground walnuts
1 cup/8 oz sugar
$\frac{1}{2}$ tsp vanilla extract (essence)
juice of half a lemon
juice of half an orange
$\frac{1}{4}$ cup/2 oz raisins
$\frac{1}{2}$ tsp ground cinnamon
$\frac{1}{2}$ cup/4 oz apricot jelly (jam)

Mix all the ingredients together in a large bowl. Preheat the oven to 350°F/Gas 4. Grease a deep baking tray. Divide the pastry into five equal pieces. Roll out the first piece of pastry and place it in the baking tray. Coat with a thick layer of plum jelly (jam). Roll out a

second piece of pastry, put on top of the first, and spread a layer of the nut filling on top. Repeat with the third and fourth pieces of pastry, spreading one with the poppy-seed filling and the other with the grated apples. Add 1 teaspoon of water and a sprinkling of sugar to the egg reserved for glazing. Roll out the remaining piece of pastry and lay on top of the grated apple. Brush with the egg glaze. Bake for approximately 40 minutes until golden. This is a special dessert for the feast of Simchat Torah.

PLUM DUMPLINGS

Makes approximately 30 dumplings

2½ cups/10 oz all-purpose (plain) flour, sifted
¾ cup/6 oz cottage cheese
3 medium-sized potatoes, peeled, boiled and grated
1 egg, beaten
1 egg yolk

½ tsp salt
1½ tbsp butter
8–10 tbsp milk
30 plums, stoned
sugar for sprinkling
melted butter and farmer's or ricotta cheese for serving

Mix all ingredients together to form a smooth dough. Roll out to a thickness of about ¼ in and cut into squares. Place a plum on each square, bring up the sides of the pastry square and press to seal and form into a round dumpling. Bring a large pan of water to the boil, drop in the dumplings, cover and cook for about 8 minutes. Then remove with a ladle and leave to drain. To serve, sprinkle with sugar, drizzle over melted butter and serve with the soft cheese on the side. A non-dairy version can be made by omitting the cottage cheese, butter and milk, and using water for the dough. The dumplings are then sprinkled with ground poppy seeds and sugar and melted goose fat is drizzled over them.

STRUDEL

(Illustrated right)

Serves 8 to 10 (2 strudels)

1 egg
⅔ cup/5 fl oz cold water
4 tbsp vegetable oil
1 tbsp wine vinegar
2½ cups/10 oz all-purpose (plain) flour, sifted

½ tsp salt
1 tsp baking powder
vegetable oil or melted butter for coating the pastry, plus extra for greasing

Beat the egg with the oil and the vinegar. Mix the flour with the salt, the baking powder and the egg mixture and add cold water. Knead for about 10 minutes to form a smooth pliable pastry. Cover with a warmed bowl for 20 minutes. Preheat the oven to 350°F/Gas 4. Place the pastry on a floured board and roll out until very thin; stretch the pastry until it is almost transparent. Brush with oil or melted butter and place the filling on one half of the pastry. Lift the pastry sheet and roll up the strudel by the edges. Transfer to a greased baking tray. Brush the pastry with oil or butter and bake for nearly 45 minutes until golden brown. Cut into thick slices while still hot and allow to cool before serving.

STRUDEL

Very few people today can bake a good strudel. Tradition has it that the noble art of strudel baking originated in Austria and was perfected in Hungary and Romania. Strudel, stretched from fine, thinly rolled out dough, filled with juicy fruit and raisins, demands a certain degree of skill in its preparation. The filling often contains apples, but cottage cheese or savoury vegetable fillings are just as good. Strudel is an excellent dish for both feast and ordinary days. It is especially apt at Sukkot when as many dishes as possible made from autumn fruit and vegetables are served.

For the apple filling
1 cup/3¼ oz breadcrumbs
1½ cup/6 oz ground
   walnuts
4 cups/2 lb apples, thinly
   sliced
2 tbsp lemon juice
1 cup/8 oz raisins
½–¾ cup/4–6 oz sugar
2 tsps cinnamon

Brush the pastry with oil or melted butter, sprinkle the breadcrumbs over one half of the pastry sheet, then spread the walnuts evenly on top. Mix the apples with the lemon juice and raisins, and spread a layer of this mixture on top of the walnuts. Mix the sugar with the cinnamon, sprinkle on top of the apples, and roll up the pastry.

For the cabbage filling
2 tbsp butter
1 onion, grated
6 cups/1½ lb finely
   chopped cabbage
2 tsp salt
½ tsp ground black
   pepper
½ cup/1½ oz
   breadcrumbs

Heat the butter in a large pan. Add the onion and cook until soft. Add the cabbage and cook for 25 minutes. Stir in the salt and pepper and leave to cool. Sprinkle the breadcrumbs on half the oiled pastry sheet, spread over the cabbage filling and roll up the pastry.
As a variation, the onion and cabbage may be fried in poultry fat, in which case make sure that no butter is used to brush the pastry.

CHANUKAH
חנוכה

Nes godol haya sham. "A great miracle occurred there." This great miracle took place in the Temple of Jerusalem in 165 BCE. It was a difficult time for the Jews who were suffering oppression at the hands of the Syrian king Antiochus Epiphanes II who tried to suppress their faith. He forbade them to study the Torah and to live in accordance with their commandments. He occupied Jerusalem and had a statue of Jupiter erected in the Holy Temple and a pig sacrificed on the altar. Not far from Jerusalem, in a small village called Modein, there lived an old priest with his five sons. The priest was Mattathias of the Hasmonean family. Mattathias and his sons gathered together a handful of fighters and went into the mountains to prepare for a revolt against Antiochus' army. After the death of Mattathias, the head of the Jewish resistance became his third son Judas who, for his extraordinary strength and courage, earned the name Maccabeus (*makabet* in Hebrew means "hammer"), and the name was passed on to his brothers. Judas Maccabeus was a brilliant leader and the Jews gained many victories under his leadership.

The decisive clash of forces came about near the town of Emmaus. Antiochus confronted the small group of Maccabees with an army of 40,000 foot-soldiers and 7,000 cavalrymen. However, in spite of such a superior enemy force, Judas, using all his wit and cunning, won the battle. The following year Antiochus sent a stronger army of 60,000 foot-soldiers and 5,000 cavalrymen to fight against the Maccabees.

Left:
Curtain, Bohemia, 1765

Right:
*Passover Haggadah,
The Jerusalem Temple,
Moravia, 1728*

Again the smaller force came away victorious. After the clash with Judas, Lysias, the prudent leader of the enemy force, recognized that the Jews would rather die than live without their faith, so he withdrew the rest of the army. King Antiochus could not bear the burden of his defeat so in desperation he threw himself into the sea. Judas Maccabeus recapturd Jerusalem and on the 25th day of Kislev in 165 BCE he rededicated the Temple and renewed Jewish worship and services. However, in the Temple only one jug was found containing pure oil required for the lighting of the eternal light in the menorah or branched candlestick. In spite of this the candlestick was lit and then a miracle occurred. There was only enough oil for barely a day, but the light burned for eight days during which time the Jews were able to secure a new supply of pure oil.

So, in commemoration of this miracle, the festival of Chanukah (i.e. "dedication"), also called the Festival of Lights, takes place every year on the 25th of Kislev. Every evening one candle is lit on a special Chanukah candelabrum. Each newly-lit candle corresponds to each new day that the eternal light burned on the menorah in the Temple. As soon as the first star appears in the sky, the entire family gathers together to participate in the ritual of lighting the Chanukah light. The blessing which is said before lighting the candles is: "Blessed art thou, O Lord our God, King of the universe, who performed miracles for our fathers in those days and at this season." The first candle to be lit is placed on the right side of the branched candlestick. On the second and subsequent evenings a new candle is added each time and this one is lit first before the others. The symbolic magnitude of the miracle increases with the

number of candles lit. The Chanukah candles are lit with the aid of a special ninth candle which is called *shammash*, "the helper". Each time the following is uttered, "These lights are sacred and we are not allowed to use them but only to gaze at them in order that we may give thanks to thy name, for thy miracles and help." The Chanukah lights are equally dear to our hearts as the lights of the Temple menorah.

When gazing into the warm, flickering flames, we are again partaking of the miracle and thanksing the Lord for all the miracles He has already carried out for us during the days of this time. Unlike other feasts, work is not forbidden on the festival of Chanukah. However, no work may be carried out while the Chanukah candles burn, so everyone can rest just as the Maccabees rested after defeating their enemies; the first letters of the word Chanukah mean "they had a rest". After lighting the Chanukah candles, the well-known song *Ma'oz Tzur Yeshuati* ("Strength, the rock of my salvation") is sung, which, in five verses, celebrates the deliverance from Egyptian slavery, Babylonian banishment, the murderous conspiracy of Haman, and finally the great Maccabean victory over the Greek enemies and the miracle which occurred at that time in the Holy Temple.

The festival of Chanukah is a time for meeting and experiencing joy together in remembrance of the past and voicing hope for the future. Fasting and elegies for the

Chanukah candlestick,
Bohemia (Prague), c. 1800

The Chanukah table

deceased are strictly forbidden. People are happy and obliging to one another, they exchange visits and hold evening parties for friends. However, those who enjoy this festival most are the children. They are happy as they receive gifts every evening, listen to fairy tales and biblical stories, in particular the apocryphal one about the Maccabees. The giving of gifts at Chanukah originates from an ancient custom which in Yiddish was called *Chanukah gelt*; children would receive money for their teachers in *cheder* (school). This tradition is still observed today yet of course now the children use the money to buy gifts for themselves. For eight whole days no one forces them to study and they are free to play. The children look forward most of all to the dreidel, in Hebrew *svivon*, the most typical game of this festival. *Svivon* means spinning-top, but it is no ordinary spinning-top. Inscribed on it are the Hebrew letters *nun, gimel, hay* and *shin,* which are the start of the words in the sentence *Nes gadol hayah sham.* The letters also stand for the Yiddish words *Nem gib, halb* and *shtell* – take, give, half and put – and so give instructions for betting on the top.

Like every Jewish festival, so Chanukah has its typical dishes: food is consumed in abundance and with great relish. The Chanukah table should contain dishes fried in oil to remind us of the miraculous oil found in the Temple. A particular favourite are doughnuts (*soofganiyot*) and potato *latkes*.

Cheese dishes are also popular at this time and symbolize another famous event of this time. They are eaten in memory of the heroic act carried out by the beautiful Judith who became the object of desire of Holofernes, the leader of Nebuchadnezzar's army. However, Judith was not only endowed with great beauty, bus also with great cunning. She fed Holofernes salted cheese and, after quenching his thirst with many cups of wine, he fell into a deep sleep. She then cut off his head. She brought it to Jerusalem to show to his soldiers and, horrified by the fate of their leader, they fled from the city.

It was lovely to sit in the twilight next to the high warm stove. The falling shadows of the firelight drew enormous and mysterious figures on the white walls of the big room.

The most beautiful evenings were on the festival of Chanukah. Impatiently we would wait for Father to return from the synagogue in the district town. We prepared a simple wooden board on the marble table and on it placed the relevant number of candles with the *shammash*. As soon as Father came home, we would have potato pancakes for supper and then the whole family would get together in the big room. Father would say a prayer in honour of the miracle which took place in the great Temple of Jerusalem where, at the time of the great victory by the Maccabees, only a little holy oil was available to keep the eternal light burning for a period of eight days. Then he would light the candles. A majestic burst of song resounded through the room with the words: *"Maos tzur yeshuosi lecha noe leshabeach tykkon beyit tefilosi veshom todo nezabeach lees tochin matbeach mitzor hamnabeach"* and even louder was the chorus *"oz egmor beshir mizmor Chanukah hamizbeach,"* so that the window shutters began to vibrate with our victorious voices. And the neighbours would say: "The Jews are celebrating their Christmas, it will soon be time for ours!" The candles flickered happily and the magic of the Chanukah evening was carried through the room. My parents, the old woman and my older sisters left after work. We, the younger children, stayed around the candles. Our neighbour Otýn slowly shuffled in and we began the Chanukah games.

There were eight candles, the *shammash* was not included. The burnt-down candle from the previous evenings went out much sooner than the rest...

KAREL LAMBERK, *Memoirs*

Drapery, Bohemia, 19th century

BEEF MEATLOAF

Serves 6 to 8

$2\frac{1}{4}$ lb ground beef
$1\frac{1}{4}$ lb smoked ground beef
2 bread rolls, soaked in water and squeezed
1 medium-sized onion, grated

2 eggs, beaten
2 egg yolks
1 tbsp goose or chicken fat
1 tsp salt
$\frac{1}{2}$ tsp ground black pepper

Preheat the oven to 350°F/Gas 4. Mix all the ingredients together and form into a loaf shape. Place in a roasting pan and pour over 1 cup/8 fl oz of water to prevent it from drying out. Roast for 1 hour basting with more water if necessary. Ground or finely chopped veal or smoked poultry meat may be used instead of the smoked beef.

POTATO PANCAKES

(Illustrated left)

Serves 4 to 5

3 cups/$1\frac{1}{2}$ lb boiled and mashed potatoes
3 tsp salt
$\frac{1}{2}$ cup/2 oz wholemeal flour
$\frac{1}{2}$ cup/2 oz potato flour

1 egg, beaten
vegetable oil or poultry fat for frying

Mix the mashed potatoes with the salt, wholemeal and potato flours and the egg. Roll out the potato mixture on a board to a thickness of approximately $\frac{1}{8}$ in and cut out shapes with a round cutter. Heat the oil or poultry fat, add the pancakes and fry. They can also be roasted, in a lightly greased dish, in a medium oven until golden. They can be coated with melted goose or poultry fat.

LATKES

On the feast of Chanukah all Jewish households are filled with the smell of traditional potato pancakes fried in oil (*latkes*, in Yiddish). The oil in which they are cooked symbolizes the small amount of oil which burned miraculously in the Temple keeping the eternal flame alight. *Latke* is also the name given to cheese scones which resemble the salted cheese which Judith was said to have served to Holofernes before killing him.

Jews probably adopted potato pancakes sometime in the seventeenth century from the Ukraine where "Kartoflani placke" were a popular side dish with Christmas goose. Instead of oil, goose fat was also used as it was abundant in the winter when geese were well fattened. This custom still survives today.

Just as with other Jewish dishes, *latkes* come in many forms, according to local or family tradition. They can be eaten on their own or with sugar, cream, yogurt apple sauce. They can be eaten throughout the day, for breakfast, lunch and the evening meal.

CHALLAH LATKES I

Makes approximately 12 pancakes

5 large potatoes, peeled and grated
1 onion, grated
4 eggs, beaten

$\frac{1}{4}$ cup/1 oz matzah meal or all-purpose (plain) flour
salt
ground black pepper
oil for frying

Mix all the ingredients together. Heat the oil and put large tablespoons of the potato mixture into the pan and immediately spread them out into thin pancakes. Fry until golden on both sides. Repeat until all the potato mixture is used up.

CHALLAH LATKES II

Serves 3 to 5

1 large challah,
  approximately 1 lb in
  weight
3 eggs, beaten
1 grated onion or 4
  crushed cloves garlic
salt
ground black pepper
oil for frying

Tear the challah into pieces, put into a large bowl and cover with water. When it is soft, squeeze out as much water as possible. Mix in the egg, onion or garlic, season and stir well. Heat the oil. Place spoonfuls of the mixture in the pan with the hot oil and fry on both sides until golden.

CHEESE LATKES

Makes approximately 12 pancakes

3 eggs, beaten
$\frac{1}{4}$ cup/2 fl oz water
2 tbsp sugar

$1\frac{1}{2}$ cups/3 oz grated hard cheese or cottage cheese
$\frac{1}{2}$ cup/2 oz all-purpose (plain) flour, sifted

3 tbsp milk
salt
ground black pepper
oil for frying
cherry jelly (jam) for serving

Mix all the ingredients together. Heat the oil. Put spoonfuls of the potato mixture into the pan and fry on both sides until golden. Serve with the cherry jam.

QUICK CHEESE BLINTZES

(Illustrated right)

Serves 6

For the batter
4 large eggs, beaten
$1\frac{1}{4}$ cups/10 fl oz milk
2 tbsp soured cream
$\frac{1}{4}$ cup/$2\frac{1}{2}$ fl oz melted butter or margarine, plus extra for greasing
1 tbsp vanilla-flavoured sugar

$1\frac{1}{3}$ cups/5 oz all-purpose (plain) flour
$1\frac{1}{4}$ tsp baking powder

For the filling
2 cups/1 lb cottage or riccota cheese
2 eggs, beaten
2–3 tbsp sugar

Preheat the oven to 375°F/Gas 5. Mix all the batter ingredients together. Pour $1\frac{1}{2}$ cups/12 fl oz of the batter into a greased roasting pan and bake for about 10 minutes. Remove from the oven. Prepare the filling by mixing all the ingredients thoroughly. Allow the cooked batter to cool very slightly, then spread the filling on top. Smooth the surface and slowly pour the remaining batter on top. Carefully replace in the oven and bake for another 40–50 minutes until the top is firm.

SOOFGANIYOT (DOUGHNUTS)

Makes approximately 25

$\frac{1}{3}$ cup/3 oz sugar

$\frac{1}{4}$ cup/$2\frac{1}{2}$ fl oz milk

$1\frac{1}{2}$ fresh yeast

1 cup/8 oz butter or margarine

4 cups/1 lb all-purpose (plain) flour, sifted, plus extra for dusting

$\frac{1}{2}$ tsp salt

4 eggs, beaten

apricot jelly (jam)

oil for deep-frying

confectioner's (icing) sugar for dusting

Add $\frac{1}{2}$ teaspoon of the sugar to the milk and heat gently until lukewarm. Crumble the yeast into the milk and leave in a warm place for about 10 minutes. Cream the butter or margarine with the sugar and mix in the flour, salt, eggs and the yeast and milk mixture. Work into a moist dough. If the dough is too dry, add a little more milk. Dust the dough with flour, cover with a teacloth and leave in a warm place for approximately 1 hour until it has risen to twice its original size. On a floured board roll out the dough to a thickness of approximately $\frac{5}{8}$ in. Cut out rounds with a pastry cutter and place a teaspoon of jelly in the centre of each round. Carefully cover with a second round of dough and seal the edges. Repeat until all the dough is used up. Cover with a teacloth and leave to rise for approximately half an hour. Heat the oil and deep-fry on both sides until golden. Remove from the oil, drain and dust with confectioner's (icing) sugar. Serve while warm.

RUGELACH

Serves 8 to 10

4 cups/1 lb all-purpose
  (plain) flour, sifted
2 tsp baking powder
2 eggs, beaten
$\frac{1}{2}$ cup/4 oz margarine,
  plus extra for greasing
$\frac{1}{2}$ cup/4 fl oz orange juice

For the filling
1 tbsp sugar
1 tsp ground cinnamon

Mix the flour with the baking powder, eggs, sugar, margarine and orange juice, and chill for 1 hour. Preheat the oven to 350°F/Gas 4. Divide the dough into four pieces and roll out each piece on a floured board to form large, thin round pancakes. Mix the sugar and cinnamon together and then sprinkle over the pancakes. Cut each round into 4 almost triangular sections, and then divide these again to make 8. Roll each piece from the outer edge to the centre of the circle, and place on a lightly greased baking tray and bake for about 20 minutes until light brown.

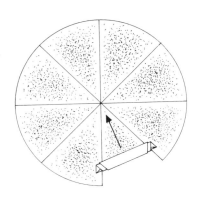

TU BISHVAT
ט״ו בשבט

The 15th of Shevat, the New Year for Trees, usually falls in late January or beginning of February. Celebrated throughout Israel and in the Diaspora, it is a festival full of joy at the planting and cultivation of trees.

The Jewish people, like all ancient cultures with deeply rooted links with the soil, have always been aware of the importance of trees to human life. The Jewish people are also symbolically regarded as an age-old tree as the Prophet Joshua said: "The days of my people are like the days of the tree. And when ye shall come into the land, and shall have planted all manner of trees for food, then ye shall count the fruit thereof..." (Lev. Chap. 19:23) – these words accompanied our forefathers during their wanderings in the wilderness.

According to the Talmud, on the day of *Tu bishvat* the first spring sap begins to flow in the trees. In the Holy Land the first signs of spring appear at this time of the year. Fruit trees begin to sprout and bud, and the landscape is lit up with the marvellous colours of blossoming almond trees. This is the time for planting young trees and it lasts until the 15th day of Adar, the feast of Purim.

The New Year for Trees is also the name given to *Rosh Hashanah ilanot* when trees are subjected to the judgement of God. According to tradition, on this day God decides which trees are to be blessed with growth throughout the year, which will bear fruit and which will dry up. In the past the custom at *Tu bishvat* was to plant

Left:
Shiviti table, detail, Bohemia

Right:
Mizrach, Slovakia, 18th century

a seedling in the ground for every child born in a family – cedars and cypresses for boys and pines for girls. When children grew up, strong branches from their trees were used to make poles for reinforcing the traditional wedding canopy or *chupa*.

This tradition continued later in the Diaspora when Jews found homes in other countries, but they did not have the same conditions for the cultivation of warmth-loving trees. In many European countries it would still be cold on the feast of *Tu bishvat* and the young seedlings would freeze in the ground, so the feast took on a different aspect. The custom was introduced for serving fruit from warmer climates, such as citrus fruits, dates, figs, raisins and almonds. These would be given to children and adults returning from the synagogue service. Boys would also take citrus fruits to school to remind them of the generosity and fertility of the trees in the land of their ancestors while listening to the biblical stories.

In Israel, the feast of *Tu bishvat* possesses an even deeper significance: the planting of trees is important to prevent soil erosion, to retain the humidity of the soil and, last but not least, to decorate the landscape of the country. In present-day Israel on *Tu bishvat* the planting of trees is accompanied by festivities, singing and dancing, and banqueting at home and in public.

In modern-day Tel Aviv, a festival takes place on this feast day which is known throughout the Jewish world. From early in the morning a blare of trumpets resounds throughout the city to summon schoolchildren to take up positions at the spots where young trees are to be planted. Older children, dressed in symbolic priest's garments, make speeches on the significance of the festival. This is then followed by a programme of songs and recitations. The event culminates in the presentation of

young tree seedlings to children. As soon as the seedlings are placed in their destined spots in pre-dug holes in the ground and carefully watered, the children hold hands and sing and dance around the young trees. The entire ceremony ends with the national anthem of Israel.

So *Tu bishvat* is often described now as the "Day of Israel". The ceremony of tree planting takes place wherever geographical and climatic conditions allow. Elsewhere this feast day is accompanied by games and ceremonies which recall the Holy Land, its history, traditions and agricultural life. The food which is served at home can be varied, but citrus fruits and nuts predominate. There is also a delicacy, a favourite among children, with a delicious smell of honey, dates and carob, sometimes referred to as Saint John's bread, named after the fruit of the Ceratonia strain of carob tree which can be traced back to biblical times. It is said that in ancient times this tree saved many a Jewish hero from starvation when in hiding to escape persecution by the enemy.

Left:
Mizrach, Bohemia, early 19th century

Right:
Mizrach, Bohemia, c. 1840

PICADILLO

Serves 6

1 tbsp vegetable oil
2¼ lb ground beef
1 onion, finely chopped
3 cloves garlic, crushed
1¼ lb tomatoes, peeled
  and chopped
2 apples, peeled and
  cubed
1 green pepper, chopped
½ cup/4 oz raisins
½ tsp chilli powder
½ tsp ground cinnamon
¼ tsp ground cloves
¼ tsp ground caraway
  seeds
½ tsp salt
¼ tsp ground black pepper
¼ cup/6 oz stuffed green
  olives
½ cup/2½ oz blanched and
  chopped almonds

Heat the oil in a large
pan. Add the meat, onion
and garlic and fry until
browned. Add the
tomatoes, apples, green
pepper, raisins, chilli
powder, spices, caraway
seeds and salt. Cover and
simmer for half an hour.
When the liquid has
evaporated, add the olives
and almonds and cook
for 1 minute to heat them
through.

BEEF CURRY WITH FRUIT

(Illustrated left)

Serves 5 to 6

2 tbsp vegetable oil
1 onion, finely chopped
1⅔ lb lean beef or lamb, cubed
1½ cups/12 fl oz water
2 tbsp lemon juice
1 tbsp curry powder
½ tsp salt
¼ tsp ground ginger
¼ tsp ground cinnamon
1¼ cups/8½ oz dried
  fruit such as apples,
  apricots and pears
½ cup/4 oz raisins
2 bananas
2 tbsp parve margarine

Heat the oil in a large pan, add the onion and fry until
browned. Add the meat and brown on all sides.
Meanwhile mix the water, lemon juice, curry powder,
salt, ginger and cinnamon together and pour into the
pan. Add the dried fruit and the raisins. Stir well, bring
to the boil, cover and simmer very slowly (about
2 hours) until the meat and fruit are soft and tender
and the sauce has thickened. Add a little water if the
curry begins to stick. Peel the bananas, slice and fry in
margarine until tender. Serve with the curry.

DRIED FRUIT AND NUT BALLS

(Illustrated left)

Makes 20 to 30 balls

- $\frac{1}{2}$ cup/4 oz dried apricots, finely chopped
- $\frac{1}{2}$ cup/4 oz pitted dates, finely chopped
- $\frac{1}{2}$ cup/4 oz dried figs, finely chopped
- $\frac{1}{2}$ cup/$2\frac{1}{2}$ oz ground walnuts
- $\frac{1}{2}$ cup/3 oz desiccated coconut
- 2 tbsp honey

Mix all the ingredients together. Form walnut-sized balls from the mixture and chill. Bring to room temperature at least half an hour before serving.

DRIED FRUIT CAKE

Serves 4 to 6

Bottom layer

- $\frac{1}{2}$ cup/4 oz margarine
- $\frac{1}{4}$ cup/2 oz sugar
- 1 cup/4 oz all-purpose (plain) flour, sifted

Top layer

- $\frac{1}{2}$ cup/2 oz all-purpose (plain) flour, sifted
- $\frac{1}{2}$ tsp baking powder
- $\frac{1}{4}$ cup/$1\frac{1}{2}$ oz demerara sugar
- 2 eggs, beaten
- 1 tsp vanilla-flavoured sugar
- $\frac{1}{2}$ cup/4 oz finely chopped dried apricots
- $\frac{1}{2}$ cup/4 oz finely chopped dried figs
- $\frac{1}{2}$ cup/$2\frac{1}{2}$ oz blanched and chopped almonds

Preheat the oven to 350°F/Gas 4. Cream the margarine with the sugar and add the flour. Press the mixture into an ungreased cake pan (tin) and bake for about 20 minutes until light brown. Meanwhile prepare the top layer: mix the flour, baking powder, demerara sugar, eggs and vanilla-flavoured sugar together. Blend well, then add the apricots, figs and chopped almonds. Spread this mixture on the partially cooked first layer, return to the oven and bake for another 25 minutes until firm and brown.

PURIM
פורים

"And Mordecai went out from the presence of the King in royal apparel of blue and white, and with a great crown of gold, and with a garment of fine linen and purple; and the city of Shushan rejoiced and was glad. The Jews had light, and gladness, and joy, and honour" (Esther Chap. 8:15, 16).

These words are heard every year in all synagogues on the festival of Purim, one of the most joyous holidays of the Jewish calendar. Jews all over the world celebrate it to commemorate the great victory over Haman, the first chamberlain and favourite of the Persian king Ahasuerus, as written in the Book of Esther. The story has a fairy-tale quality: during the reign of Ahasuerus there lived in Shushan, the capital city of the Kingdom of Persia, a Jew by the name of Mordecai who had a niece of extraordinary beauty and wisdom. She was so beautiful that King Ahasuerus made her his wife after banishing Queen Vashti. Another important figure in this story was Haman, an arrogant and domineering man, full of anger and hatred for all Jews. He enjoyed particular favour with King Ahasuerus who made him more important than all the princes, so that everyone had to kneel and bow down before him: everyone, that is, except Mordecai who, as a Jew, refused to do so. This served as a good enough excuse for the treacherous

Left:
Shiviti table, Bohemia, 19th century

Right:
Scroll of Esther, Bohemia, 17th–18th century

Scroll of Esther, Bohemia, 18th century

Haman to openly attack all the Jews in the Kingdom of Persia. He issued an edict which ruled that on the 13th day of Adar all Persian Jews were to be killed. This date was chosen by drawing lots. This is how the name Purim came because the Hebrew word for lot is *pur*. The fate of the Jews would have been sealed had it not been for Mordecai and Esther who with her wit and courage saved them at the last moment. As soon as Mordecai told her what was going to happen, she prepared a banquet and invited Haman to attend. When all the guests had drunk wine and were in sufficiently high spirits she stood before the King and told him of the danger threatening all the Jews in his kingdom asking him to save her and her people's lives. When the King asked who was responsible for this terrible act, Esther pointed to Haman. Ahasuerus' anger knew no bounds and so the treacherous Haman ended his miserable life on the gallows that he had prepared earlier for Mordecai. Mordecai was bestowed with all the royal privileges and became the second most powerful man in the kingdom after Ahasuerus.

However, the story does not end with the death of Haman. Esther also asked the King to allow Mordecai to send letters in his name throughout the land calling on the

Jews to take revenge on their enemies. So it came to pass that on the 13th of Adar, precisely on the day which was to be their last, it was the Jews who slew their enemies instead. The next day the Jews rejoiced in their salvation. However, a battle still raged in the city of Shushan and celebrations could not take place until the following day, called Shushan Purim. For this reason Purim is commemorated on both the 14th and 15th of Adar.

Purim holds a unique position among Jewish holidays. It is not a holiday commanded by God. All its customs develop from a story in which there is no mention of the Lord's name. It was not God but Mordecai the Jew who charged all the Jews in the Kingdom of Persia "to keep the fourteenth day of the month of Adar, and the fifteenth day of the same, yearly ... make them days of feasting and joy, and of sending portions one to another, and gifts to the poor." Each year these words are fulfilled with the most beautiful customs of Purim handed on from generation to generation. A Jew is never left alone to mourn his sorrow but always relives his joy and sorrow with others. This is true of all holidays, including Purim. So, Purim is a holiday of "feasting and joy" and, therefore, of food and drink, so Jews bring joy to their loved ones by sending them something good which they have prepared for the festive table. The gifts mentioned by Mordecai in his message comprise at least two portions of cooked food, one made

Mizrach, Slovakia, early 19th century

Scroll of Esther, Moravia, early 19th century

from flour and the other of fruit. It is from this that the Hebrew name for this custom *shalahmanot* originates: in English this means "the sending of portions" (from the Hebrew *shalah*, to send, and *manot*, portion). Festive food used to be sent on beautiful dishes covered in colourful, richly embroidered cloths. Today it is sent in somewhat more prosaic cardboard boxes made especially for this purpose. Of course, it is not only food made of flour and fruit that is sent. Everyone also likes to include something of the typical Purim sweetmeats such as the fearful-looking gingerbread figures of Haman, their Sephardic equivalent of "Haman's ears" or the popular Ashkenazi *Hamantaschen*, triangular cakes filled with poppy seed (in Yiddish *mohn* = poppy-seed, *taschen* = pocket) which should recall Haman's three-pointed hat or his pocket full of bribes. *Mohn Kichlach* are also sent. These represent the sweetmeat sprinkled with poppy seed that Esther ate at the court of King Ahasuerus instead of the non-kosher delicacies.

Besides sending gifts to each other, Mordecai also told the Jews not to forget about the poor. At the time of Purim every Jew should donate money to at least two poor people near to where he lives so that they too can share the joy of the festival.

It is difficult to describe on paper the unique magic of the feast of Purim. The rejoicing at Purim is colourful and unrestrained, full of lively teasing and practical jokes. Everyone rejoices and displays their joy openly and without restraint. Almost everything is permitted on this day. Children and adults put on fancy-dress costumes and masks and walk along streets playing tricks on everyone they meet, even on the rabbi. Scenes, or sometimes the whole tale, are acted out from the biblical story of Queen Esther. No one is allowed to stay sober. Wine is an integral part of all Jewish celebrations because it brings joy and gladness to the soul. At Purim wine has an additional symbolic role because it contributed to the defeat of Haman. It was wine that caused

the drunk Ahasuerus to banish Queen Vashti and elevate Esther to her position. Esther served wine at her famous banquet which led to the betrayal of Haman. It is still drunk in large quantities today. The Talmud states that the right state of mind at Purim is attained only when everyone has drunk enough wine and can no longer tell you who was Mordecai and who Haman. A great carnival takes place each year in Jerusalem, which is called *Ad lo yade* (in Hebrew meaning "until he did not know").

On Purim the Book of Esther is read in all synagogues. On the eve a festive meals is served on the return from the service. Countless dishes are prepared at Purim and each one of these symbolically reminds us of one of the figures or events of the Old Testament story. The meal should include a turkey whose Hebrew name is *tarnegol hodu* (meaning "Indian cock"), a reminder of stupid King Ahasuerus who "reigned from India even unto Ethiopia". Among the specialities served on Purim, it is a custom to serve a sweet and sour dish. This allows us to re-live the great sorrow which overcame all the Persian Jews when they learned of their planned destruction and then experience the great joy from the defeat of the evil Haman, and finally from the end of all their woes and sufferings.

And now, that you know my family a little better, you can understand my pride in them and my enjoyment of their company, especially when the holidays come around. For instance, the *Purim sudah*, when all my children and grandchildren gather about the table and we make a blessing over the big shiny *Purim* load covered with saffron and studded with raisins, and my wife serves the good strong spicy fish with horseradish and the rich soup with the long yellow noodles in it. And we take a drop of something, if the Lord permits – a glass of port or cherry wine, if we have it, and if we don't, a sip of ordinary brandy is welcome too. And we sing in a chorus. I begin the song and the children come in on the refrain and the little ones, the grandchildren, pipe the second refrain in their high shrill voices.

SHOLOM ALEICHEM, *Tovye the Dairyman*

Kasrilevka had not seen such a warm, mild *Purim* for a long time... A lucky thing that almost nobody in town had money for *matzos* yet, or you might have thought it was Passover and not *Purim*.

The *shalachmones* which Red Nechama carried consisted of a large *hamantash* filled with poppy-seed, two cushion cakes – one open-faced and filled with *farfel*, the other round and handsomely decorated on both sides – a sugar cookie with a plump raisin stuck right in the middle of it, a large square of *torte*, and big slice of nut-bread, two small cherub cakes, and a large piece of spice cake which had turned out better than any that Zelda had ever made. Whether the flour was exceptionally good this year or the honey purer, or whether the cake had baked just long enough, or she had beaten it more than usual, it doesn't matter. It was light and puffy as a feather cushion.

SHOLOM ALEICHEM, *Tovye the Dairyman*

All the neighbours sent *shalachmones* – Purim gifts. From early afternoon the messengers kept coming. They brought wine, mead, oranges, cakes, and cookies. One generous man sent a tin of sardines; another, smoked salmon; a third, sweet-and-sour fish. They brought apples carefully wrapped in tissue paper, dates, figs – anything you could think of. The table was heaped with delicacies. Then came the masked mummers, with helmets on their heads and carrying cardboard shields and swords, all covered with gold or silver paper.

For Krochmalna, Purim was a grand carnival. The street was filled with maskers and bearers of gifts. It smelled of cinnamon, saffron and chocolate, of freshly baked cakes and all sorts of sweets and spices whose names I did not know. The sweetshops sold cookies in the shapes of King Ahasuerus, Haman the Wicked, the chamberlain Harbona, Queen Vashti, and Vaizatha, the tenth son of Haman. It was good to bite off Haman's leg, or to swallow the head of Queen Esther. And the noisemakers kept up a merry clamor, in defiance of all the Hamans of all the ages.

ISAAC BASHEVIS SINGER, *In My Father's Court*

MUSHROOM SOUP WITH GROATS

Serves 8

$8\frac{1}{2}$ oz peeled and chopped tomatoes
1 small onion, finely chopped
2 tbsp finely chopped celery
1 tbsp salt
1 tbsp finely chopped fresh parsley
$\frac{1}{4}$ cup beans, soaked overnight
$\frac{1}{4}$ cup groats or barley, rinsed
1 small carrot, chopped
1 cup/4 oz dried mushrooms, soaked overnight and finely chopped
1 tbsp freshly chopped dill
$\frac{1}{4}$ tsp ground black pepper
$4\frac{1}{2}$ cups/$1\frac{3}{4}$ pints water

Put the tomatoes, onion, celery, parsley, beans, groats, mushrooms and water in a large pan and cook over a medium heat for $1\frac{1}{2}$ hours. Then add the carrot, the salt and pepper and the dill and cook for approximately half an hour until the carrot is soft. If the soup is too thick add some more water and boil for a few minutes longer.

PEA "SAUSAGES"

(Illustrated right)

Makes approximately 20

3 cups/$1\frac{1}{2}$ lb yellow peas
8 slices white bread, crusts removed
2 eggs, beaten
3 cloves garlic, crushed
$\frac{1}{4}$ tsp cayenne pepper
1–2 tsp salt
$\frac{1}{4}$ tsp ground black pepper
oil for frying

Sort the peas, wash, cover with water and leave overnight. The next day, boil for about 20 minutes, then leave to cool. Mince the peas with the bread, then mix in the eggs, garlic, cayenne pepper, salt and black pepper. Chill the mixture for an hour, then form into thick fingers about 2 in long. Heat the oil in a pan and fry the pea "sausages" until crisp. Serve warm with mustard or ketchup.

BUCKWHEAT

Serves 3

1 cup/8 oz buckwheat
1 egg, beaten
2 tbsp vegetable oil
1 onion, finely chopped
2 tbsp finely chopped
  parsley
1¼ lb freshly chopped,
  fried mushrooms or
  2 cups/4 oz dried
  mushrooms
2 cups/16 fl oz chicken
stock or water
1 tsp salt
½ tsp ground black pepper
¼ tsp cayenne pepper

Mix the buckwheat with the egg in a bowl and leave for 1 hour. Heat the oil in a large pan, add the onion and parsley and fry until the onion begins to brown. Add the mushrooms and continue to fry for a few minutes. Stir in the buckwheat and fry gently for 5 minutes, stirring constantly. Pour in the stock or water, add the salt, cayenne and black pepper, cover and simmer for approximately 20 minutes until the liquid evaporates and the buckwheat is soft and tender. Be careful not to let it dry out. If you are using dried mushrooms, leave them to soak first for at least 2 hours in warm water. Drain, then fry until soft and chop up. Buckwheat cooked like this can be served on its own or can be used as a pastry filling. Served with an equal quantity of wide cooked noodles, it is called *Kasha varnishkes*.

POTATO PARCELS STUFFED WITH MEAT

Makes 15 to 20 parcels

For the dough
2¼ lb mashed potato
1 large egg, beaten
6 tbsp wholemeal flour
2 tbsp potato flour
1 tbsp salt

For the filling
1¼ lb ground beef
1 tsp salt
½ tsp freshly ground black
   pepper
1 medium-sized onion,
   finely chopped
4–5 cloves garlic, finely
   chopped
1 sweet pepper, finely
   chopped

For the coating
1 large egg beaten with
   1 tsp water
matzah meal or
   breadcrumbs for coating
oil for frying

To prepare the filling, season the meat with the salt and pepper and fry gently with the onion, garlic and chopped pepper until it is browned and the pepper is soft. Mix all the dough ingredients together. Knead the dough on a floured board and roll it out to a thickness of approximately ¼ in. Cut into squares. Place 1 tablespoon of the filling on each square, fold over the edges and press to seal firmly. Glaze the triangles with the egg, and dip into the matzah meal or breadcrumbs. Heat the oil and fry on both sides until golden.

TURKEY SCHNITZELS WITH FRUIT

Serves 4

1–1¾ lb skinned and
  boned turkey breast

1 tsp salt

½ tsp ground ginger

1 tsp ground white pepper

¼ tsp paprika

2 tbsp white wine or juice
  of 1 lemon

4 tbsp vegetable oil

1 small bunch grapes

1 orange, peeled and
  chopped

½ cup/4 oz blanched
  chopped almonds, to
  garnish

Cut the turkey meat into 12–16 pieces. To tenderize them, place them between sheets of greaseproof paper and beat them with a tenderizing hammer or rolling pin. When they are slightly flattened, coat with the salt, ginger and ground white pepper and paprika. Drizzle over the white wine or lemon juice and half the oil, and chill for at least 1 hour. Heat the remaining oil. Add the turkey schnitzels and cook until the meat is tender. Add the grapes and orange pieces and leave to simmer for a little while longer, about 8–10 minutes. Scatter over the almonds to garnish and serve immediately.

STUFFED TURKEY

Serves 6

$2\frac{1}{4}$ lb turkey breasts, tenderized
1 tsp salt
$\frac{1}{2}$ tsp ground black pepper

For the stuffing

2 tbsp vegetable oil
1 onion, finely chopped
1 cup farfel (see page 69)
1 cup/8 fl oz stock
1 tsp salt
$\frac{1}{2}$ tsp ground black pepper
$\frac{1}{4}$ tsp freshly grated nutmeg
$\frac{1}{2}$ cup/$1\frac{1}{2}$ oz freshly chopped parsley
1 carrot, grated
$\frac{1}{2}$ cup/1 oz celery, finely chopped

Preheat the oven to 350°F/Gas 4. To prepare the stuffing heat the oil in a large pan and fry the onion until soft. Add the farfel and cook for 5 minutes. Pour over the stock, season with the salt and pepper, add the nutmeg, parsley, carrot and celery and simmer for 5 minutes. Remove from the heat and allow to cool slightly. Season the turkey breasts with salt and pepper, spread over the stuffing and roll them up. Wrap each one in silver foil or tie with string. Roast for about 1 hour until the meat is tender. If you are not using silver foil, baste with water or stock during the cooking time.

KNISHES

Serves 4 to 6

$2\frac{1}{2}$ cup/10 oz all-purpose
   (plain) flour, sifted
1 tsp baking powder
$\frac{1}{2}$ tsp salt
2 eggs
$\frac{2}{3}$ cup/5 fl oz vegetable oil,
   plus extra for coating
   and greasing
2 tbsp water

For the meat filling
$\frac{1}{2}$ cup/1 oz finely chopped
   onion
2 tbsp chicken fat or
   vegetable oil
$1\frac{1}{2}$ cups/$2\frac{1}{2}$ oz finely
   chopped cooked beef
1 egg, beaten
1 tsp salt
$\frac{1}{4}$ tsp ground black pepper

Mix the flour, baking powder and salt in a large bowl. Beat the eggs with the oil. Make a hollow in the flour mixture and pour in the eggs. Mix well to form a dough. Divide into two halves and roll out each half until very thin. Lightly brush with oil and cut out rounds approximately 2 in in diameter.

Preheat the oven to 375°F/Gas 5. Mix together all the filling ingredients and place 1 teaspoon of the filling in the centre of each pastry round. Fold the edges towards the middle, leaving a small triangle-shaped gap in the centre. The filling should just be visible. Bake on a greased baking tray for about 35 minutes until golden.

POTATO KNISHES WITH LIVER

Serves 3 to 4

For the pastry

2 cups/4 oz mashed potato

2 eggs, beaten

$\frac{1}{2}$ cup/2 oz wholemeal flour

1 tbsp potato flour

1 onion, grated

2 tbsp poultry fat or vegetable oil, plus extra for greasing

1 tsp salt

$\frac{1}{4}$ tsp ground black pepper

For the filling

1 cup/8 oz finely chopped cooked poultry or beef liver, or 1 cup/8 oz cooked ground beef

1 egg, beaten with 2 tsp water

$\frac{1}{2}$ tsp salt

$\frac{1}{4}$ tsp ground black pepper

Preheat the oven to 350°F/Gas 4. Mix the potato, eggs, wholemeal and potato flours, the onion, fat or oil, salt and pepper on a board and work into a firm dough. To prepare the filling, combine all the ingredients and mix well to form a soft mixture. Pull of small portions of the pastry and form into pyramids approximately 1 in high. Make a hollow in each pyramid and press 1 teaspoon of filling into the centre of each hollow. Seal the filling inside by pressing the pastry over the opening. Glaze the knishes with the egg and place on a well-greased baking sheet. Bake for approximately 20 minutes until golden.

BEEF WITH LENTILS AND RICE

Serves 4

1 cup/8 oz lentils
2 tbsp vegetable oil
$2\frac{1}{4}$ lb lean beef, cubed
2 onions, finely chopped
2 tsp salt
$\frac{1}{4}$ tsp ground black
  pepper
4 cups/$1\frac{2}{3}$ pints boiling
  water
$\frac{1}{2}$ cup/4 oz long-grain
  rice

Soak the lentils in cold water for an hour. Heat the oil in a pan and add the meat and onion. Fry until browned. Add the lentils, salt, pepper and boiling water. Stir well, cover and leave to simmer for $1\frac{1}{2}$ hours until the meat is tender. Then add the rice and cook for a further 25 minutes. Serve with pickled gherkins.

QUEEN ESTHER SWEETMEATS

Makes about 45 biscuits

$\frac{1}{2}$ cup/4 oz sugar

$\frac{1}{2}$ cup/4 oz butter or margarine, plus extra for greasing

1 egg, beaten

1 tbsp water

$\frac{1}{2}$ tsp vanilla extract (essence)

2 cups/8 oz all-purpose (plain) flour, sifted

$\frac{1}{2}$ tsp baking powder

$\frac{1}{4}$ cup/1 oz poppy seeds

Cream the sugar and butter in a large bowl, add the egg, water and vanilla extract (essence). Mix the flour with the baking powder and add to the bowl. Stir in the poppy seeds. Work into a very firm pastry, wrap in silver foil and leave to chill for several hours. Preheat the oven to 350°F/Gas 4. On a floured board roll out to a thickness of about $\frac{1}{2}$ in and cut out various shapes. Bake on a lightly greased baking tray for 10–15 minutes until golden brown.

HAMAN-TASCHEN

Makes 20 pieces

For the pastry

$\frac{1}{2}$ cup/4 oz soft margarine
    or butter, plus extra for
    greasing
$\frac{1}{4}$ cup/3 oz demerara
    sugar
$\frac{3}{4}$ cup/3 oz honey
$2\frac{1}{2}$ cups/10 oz all-purpose
    (plain) flour, sifted
1 tsp baking powder
$\frac{1}{2}$ tsp baking soda
    (bicarbonate of soda)
2 large eggs, beaten
1 tsp vanilla extract
    (essence)

For an alternative version of the pastry

$\frac{1}{4}$ cup/5 oz margarine
$\frac{1}{2}$ cup/4 oz sugar
1 egg, beaten
3 tbsp water or milk
$\frac{1}{2}$ tsp vanilla extract
    (essence)
$2\frac{1}{2}$–3 cups/10–12 oz plain
    flour, sifted

For the nut filling

1 cup/5 oz ground
    walnuts
1 cup/8 oz sugar
$\frac{1}{2}$ tsp vanilla extract
    (essence)
juice of half an orange
$\frac{1}{4}$ cup/2 oz raisins
$\frac{1}{2}$ tsp ground cinnamon
$\frac{1}{2}$ cup/$2\frac{1}{2}$ oz orange or
    apricot jelly

For the plum jelly

2 cups/8 oz plum jelly
    (jam)
juice of half an orange
$\frac{1}{2}$ cup/$2\frac{1}{2}$ oz ground
    almonds or walnuts

For the poppy-seed filling

$\frac{1}{4}$ cup/2 fl oz water
1 tbsp rum
$1\frac{1}{2}$ cups/8 oz ground
    poppy seeds
1 egg white
$\frac{3}{4}$ cup/6 oz sugar
$\frac{1}{2}$ tsp vanilla extract
juice of half a lemon

juice of half an orange
1 cup/8 oz raisins
$\frac{3}{4}$ tsp ground
    cinnamon
1 cup/5 oz apricot or
    raspberry jelly (jam)
$\frac{3}{4}$ cup/2 oz margarine

First make one of the
fillings. For the poppy-
seed filling mix the water
and the rum in a pan and
bring to the boil. Lower
the heat slightly and,
stirring constantly, add
the ground poppy seeds,
the egg white, sugar,
vanilla extract (essence),
lemon and orange juice,

raisins and cinnamon. Heat this mixture for 5 minutes, stirring constantly. Then mix in the jelly (jam) and the margarine and heat until combined and the margarine has melted. Remove from the heat, allow to cook then chill to firm.

For the other filling, simply mix the ingredients. To make the pastry, cream the margarine or butter, sugar and honey in a large bowl. Mix the flour with the baking powder and baking soda, and add to the bowl. Add the eggs and vanilla extract (essence) and work all the ingredients into a smooth pastry. Wrap in silver foil and chill for 2–3 hours. Preheat the oven to 375°F/Gas 5. Roll out the pastry to a thickness of approximately $\frac{1}{4}$ in. Cut into squares. Place 1 teaspoon of the filling on each square, then fold the pastry into triangles pressing the edges of the pastry together firmly. Place on a greased baking tray and bake for about 20 minutes until golden. Alternatively, the pastry can be cut into rounds of about 3 inch in diameter. The filling should be placed in the centre and the edges folded over. Bake as above.

BUTTER CAKES WITH CINNAMON

Makes approximately 20 cakes

1 cup/8 oz butter, plus extra for greasing

1 cup/8 oz sugar
2 cups/8 oz all-purpose (plain) flour, sifted
$\frac{1}{3}$ cup/3 oz ground mixed nuts or almonds
cinnamon, for dusting

Preheat the oven to 350°F/Gas 4. Cream the butter with the sugar. Gradually add the flour and then the nuts. Work into a smooth pastry and form egg-sized balls. Pat into cake shapes, but be careful not to flatten too much. Place well apart on a greased baking tray and dust with cinnamon. Bake for approximately 25 minutes. The cakes should remain white but be firm to the touch.

PASSOVER
פסח

"Why is this night different from all other nights? On all other nights we eat bread, but on this night only matzah. On all other nights we eat all kinds of herbs, but on this night only bitter herbs. On all other nights we do not even dip once, but on this night twice. On all other nights we can eat either sitting or reclining, but on this night we all recline." This is said by the youngest of the family at the festive seder meal on the first night of Passover – Pessach in Hebrew. It is at this time that the whole Jewish world recalls one of the most important events of its history: the deliverance from Egyptian bondage and the beginning of a new, free life. In Hebrew the word Pesach means "to pass over" and refers to that memorable night when the Lord went through the land of Egypt killing all the firstborn; however, He passed over the houses of the Israelites and saved them from the destruction for which the whole of Egypt was destined.

At the festival of Passover all Jews experience the exodus from Egypt as their ancestors did in reality 3,000 years ago. They relive those events, suffer the bitterness of bondage and the sweetness of redemption. As with all Jewish festivals, Passover is a complicated symbolic ritual in which even the least apparent things are significant. But this festival clearly differs from the others. The main sacred ceremony is not bound by a service in a synagogue but takes place at home when all the members of the family including the youngest child sit down to the seder evening meal. However, let us start at the beginning: before this longed-for moment arrives, a great many things must be done and prepared. It is no coincidence that Jews have many occassions on which to celebrate the fulfilment of God's commandments. For Passover, the most important commandment must be fulfilled before the beginning of the actual festival, 14th of Nisan, after sunset.

Passover is also called the feast of the unleavened bread. In the second Book of Moses we all read that unleavened bread was eaten by the Jews at God's commandment on the last night before their deliverance from Egypt (Ex. Chap. 12:15). However, when they had to leave quickly they had no time to prepare food for the journey and so they only took the dough which had not had time to rise; on their journey they baked unleavened bread from this dough (Ex. Chap. 12:39). God also commanded all the Israelites to celebrate this day for all generations in memory of their deliverance from Egypt. "Seven days shall ye eat unleaved bread; even the first day ye shall put away leaven out of your houses: for whosoever eateth leavened bread from the first day until the seventh day, that soul shall be cut off from Israel" (Ex. Chap. 12:15). This commandment has been observed ever since. In all Jewish households all that is leavened is sought out before the start of Passover so it may be burned the following day.

"Leaven" in Hebrew is called *chametz*, "unleavened" bread is called *matzah*. These words are closely related just as the leavened and unleavened dough they describe. However, the light and risen dough looks and tastes far better than the simple and bland-tasting *matzah*. For this reason, *chametz* is regarded as the symbol of arrogance, pride and the tendency towards evil which is a constant source of temptation for our soul, luring us towards wordly pleasures and transitory values. In biblical times, Egypt was the embodiment of arrogance and idolatry. "Who is the Lord, that

Left:
Breaking the matzah,
Spain, 1320–1330

Seder meal, Germany, 15th century

Passover Haggadah, Searching for chametz, Moravia, 1728

I should obey his voice to let Israel go? I know not the Lord, neither will I let Israel go" (Es. Chap. 5:2), replied the Pharaoh in answer to Moses' and Aaron's request. The only God the Egyptians worshipped was wealth and their only desire was to rule over the greatest number of slaves. The Jews who were under Egyptian captivity for 430 years were forcibly affected by this environment. So that the Jews in Egypt could be saved from the destruction of all the firstborn in the land and become a free people again, serving only their own God, they had first to be cleansed of all the evil which had penetrated their souls. The use of *matzah* can be understood as a symbolic spiritual form of purification before entering a new life. On the other hand, *chametz* is connected with the past life of lies and bondage. So, at Passover not a single piece of *chametz* may remain either in our possession or in our soul. Only then are we able to fully savour the joy of regained freedom. Rabbi Chaim Vital compares in the scripture *Hakavanot* the first 13 days of the month of Nisan to the first 13 years of life. On the eve of the first day of the festival every man must fulfil the commandment of looking for *chametz*. Good then enters his life which fills him with the strength to reveal and destroy the evil that is rooted in his soul.

All leavened bread made of wheat, barley, oats, spelt and rice flour as well as all other leavened food and drink are considered to be *chametz*. Ashkenazi Jews also in-

Rolling pin for matzot, Bohemia, 18th–19th century

clude all species of beans, rice, millet, maize, peanuts and sunflower seeds as *chametz*. *Chametz* is normally searched for on the eve of the 13th of Nisan and this is done thoroughly. The entire house must be searched, even the places where there is no *chametz*. It is the search rather than the discovery that is important. The whole house must be searched even if there is not a single grain of bread to be found. However, so that the search is not altogether fruitless, the tradition of hiding several pieces of *chametz* in various parts of the house is upheld. According to Rabbi Isaac Luria there should be at least 10 of these pieces. All the *chametz* found must be carefully put in one place to be burnt the following day. In spite of a thorough search, the possibility should be taken into account that at least one piece has been forgotten; since removing *chametz* means fully relinquishing it – i.e. removing it from one's property and mind – after ending the search the following words are said: "All leaven in my possession which I have seen or not seen, as well as all unleaved bread which I have removed or not removed, may it now be considered the dust of the earth." These words are then repeated on the 14th of Nisan after the burning of all the *chametz*. It is then forbidden to eat *chametz* or make use of it after the 14th of Nisan. "You shall not eat any *chametz*," states the Torah. These words which relate to the Passover sacrifice are traditionally interpreted as a ban on the use of *chametz* from the moment when it was permitted to kill the sacrificial lamb, i.e. after noon on the 14th of Nisan.

Seder bowls, Austria (Vienna), late 19th century

The use of the Passover kitchen utensils is closely connected with the removal of the *chametz*. Many Jewish households possess special, if possible, the most luxurious and festive utensils for Passover; these are not used at any other time of the year. However, it does not matter if a family does not possess a separate set of utensils. Many everyday utensils can be used during Passover, but they must be cleaned and ritually purified first to remove any trace of *chametz*. The method of purification varies depending on the material and construction of the utensil and the way in which it has been used.

On the 14th of Nisan carrying out work for personal gain is forbidden. Our wise men believe that we cannot be successful in any work we undertake on this day. However, this does not apply to the preparations for the seder meal which begins shortly after sunset. Yet, the firstborn sons of Jewish families spend this day differently. For them the 14th of Nisan is a day of fasting in remembrance of the deliverance of the sons of the Israelites from death for which all the firstborn of Egypt were destined.

Passover Haggadah,
Ma nishtane, *Moravia, 1728*

Below:
Passover cup, Bohemia, 1860

Below right:
Passover cup, Bohemia,
1942–1945

The seder meal is a home service. Instead of sitting in the synagogue, we sit comfortably leaning at the festive seder table. All that we say, do and eat has one objective: to re-live all the trouble and anguish throughout 26 generations of bondage and to relish fully the joy of strenuously recovered freedom. In this way joy is constantly mixed with sorrow, pride with humility, the sweetness of deliverance with the bitterness of bondage. The seder ceremony may be compared to a marvellous and intricate mosaic in which each stone is placed in a particular spot, together forming a complete and harmonious pattern. It is a sacred ritual consisting of many individual acts coming in a firmly defined and unchanging order (in Hebrew the word *seder* means "order"). No act may be left out, each has its substance and significance. The acts are symbols which speak in the same language to Jews all over the world, bridging the gap of time separating them from their ancestors and uniting them in the feeling of solidarity and pride in their common origin and destiny.

Food plays a decisive part in seder symbolism. The most important commandments which are given for Passover by the Torah apply directly to food. "Observe the month of Abib and keep the passover unto the Lord thy God: for in the month of Abib the Lord thy God brought thee forth out of Egypt by night. Thou shalt therefore sacrifice the passover unto the Lord thy God, of the flock and the herd, in the place which the Lord shall choose to place his name there. Thou shalt eat no leavened bread with it" (Deut. Chap. 16:1–3). With these words thy Lord commands his people to commemorate annually the memory of deliverance out of the land of Egypt with the Passover sacrifice of the lamb which he told all the Israelites in Egypt to kill on the eve of the last night before deliverance. On this night they ate its meat with unleavened bread and bitter herbs, they took its blood and spread it on their door frames as a sign for the Lord to pass over their houses when he killed all the firstborn. These commandments were to be carried out for as long as the Holy Temple existed in Jerusalem. In biblical times Passover was one of the pilgrimage feasts. All Jews living up to 30 days' distance from Jerusalem carried out a festive pilgrimage to the Holy Temple to place the Passover sacrifice on its altar and celebrate the memory

Matzah cover, eastern Europe, 1861

of deliverance from Egypt with a grand feast consisting of matzot, bitter herbs, *charoset*, the Passover lamb and a sacrifice called *chagiga* (i.e. the sacrifice of peace). The meat from this sacrifice was the main course because the Passover lamb could not be eaten to satisfy hunger but only for fulfilling God's commandment. The Temple has been long since destroyed so we can no longer bring to the Lord the Passover sacrifice nor the sacrifice of peace, but both still appear in symbolic form on the seder table. The following symbols appear on the seder plate: a bone, an egg, bitter herbs, charoset and green herbs. A roasted lamb bone represents the Passover sacrifice. This is placed in the top right-hand corner; the sacrifice of peace is represented by a boiled or baked egg in its shell which is placed on the left at the same level as the bone. The lamb bone and the egg remind us of the Temple ritual and also express the hope of an early rebuilding of the Temple of Jerusalem. Boiled eggs are also usually served in salted water during the meal as a symbol of the weeping over the destroyed Temple. According to the Darchei Moshe the first day of Passover comes on the same day in the week as the fast on the 9th day of the month of Av which is the anniversary of this sad event. Apart from the joy of deliverance we therefore also feel sadness for the destruction of the Temple on whose altar our ancestors laid the Passover lamb.

The bone and the eggs also symbolize the main heroes of those events, the interpreters of God's commandments, Moses and Aaron, who are not mentioned otherwise during the entire evening because this feast is one of thanksgiving to the Lord for all the wonders and miracles he worked for us. The commentator Rambam believes that the Passover lamb symbolizes the idolatry of the Egyptians for whom the

Above:
Passover Haggadah, ritual sheet, Moravia, 1728

Above right:
Passover Haggadah, the ten Egyptian plagues, Moravia, 1728

Below:
Passover Haggadah, Kiddush, Moravia, 1728

sheep was a sacred animal and could not be killed. By killing the lamb, the Israelites were purified of the pagan cult and strengthened their faith in one God. According to this interpretation, the egg on the seder plate could also be of similar importance: in Egypt all dishes coming from living animals were forbidden for religious reasons.

The third object on the plate, on the top of an imaginary triangle, under the bone and the egg, there are the bitter herbs, *maror* in Hebrew. Their bitter taste reminds us of the suffering of the Jews under Egyptian bondage. Rabbinical tradition recognizes the following species of bitter vegetables for use as *maror*: endive, chervil, horseradish or lettuce; the most suitable is considered to be the lettuce which has a sweet taste but then turns bitter on the tongue (although many households use horseradish). This is what life was like for the Israelites in Egypt. In the beginning they lived in relatively favourable conditions, but later the Egyptians "made their lives miserable with hard labour". Despite even the greatest oppression, they never stopped hoping for salvation. So at the seder meal we do not forget about that small spark of hope shining in the deepest darkness. *Maror* is not eaten on its own but is soaked in sweet *charoset* which lessens its bitter taste.

Charoset is another traditional seder dish and is the fourth symbol on the seder plate. It is placed lower down than the bone and further to the right. *Charoset* is the only seder dish which has a sweet taste. It is a mixture of grated apples, raisins, nuts and almonds which are mixed with red wine. It looks like the clay from which Jews made bricks for Pharaoh. It is the symbol of the apple tree under which Jewish women secretly gave birth to their children to protect them from the Egyptians. Red wine is added to *charoset* and that is blood, the blood of circumcision, the blood of the Passover sacrifice and also the blood of the Jewish boys murdered by Pharaoh. So life is an integral part of death, hope and desperation. Nothing sweet is not entirely sweet, just as every bitterness promises future sweetness.

Under the egg, but more to the right and at the same level as the *charoset,* is the *karpas. Karpas* holds a special position in the seder ceremony. It is any non-bitter vegetable; potatoes, carrots or parsley are normally used. It may be cooked or raw. We eat this vegetable straight after saying the Kiddush at the very beginning of the meal. Before this we say the traditional blessing "Blessed art Thou, O Lord our God, King of the Universe, who createst the fruit of the earth". This blessing also applies to the *maror* which we shall eat later. *Maror* brings forth such a bitter memory that we would rather say the obligatory blessing at another point. *Karpas* enables us to do this. It is with sweet *karpas* that we begin the seder meal because we also want to be reminded of the fact that the Lord prepared our salvation before the beginning of Egyptian bondage.

Under the *charoset* and *karpas* at the other point of the triangle, we place *chazeret* (or lettuce) which has the same meaning as *maror*.

Also on the seder table is the unleavened bread – three crisp white matzot wrapped in a special cover with partitions which separate each one. Unleavened bread was the food of our ancestors in the difficult times of Egyptian bondage, the last night before deliverance and at the beginning of the new free life. As slaves of the Pharaoh in Egypt, the Israelites had to work all the time and there was no time to prepare any other food. On the last night spent in bondage, they ate matzot and bitter herbs with the Passover lamb, and when they left Egypt in great haste, they had no time to take with them anything else other than the unleavened dough from which they baked unleavened bread in the Sinai desert. Just like the other seder dishes, matzot also bring to mind both the most sorrowful and the happiest moments of our past. They are the bread of our poverty and our deliverance.

While two loaves of *challah* are enough for the Sabbath and other festivals, three matzot are needed for seder. The top matzah is called Cohen, the middle Levi and the bottom Israel. The father breaks the middle matzah into two unequal parts; everyone at the meal eats from the smaller part during the seder to fulfil the commandment for this night of eating unleavened bread, while the large part is retained before the start of the seder meals as the *afikomen,* the part which is hidden later. Three matzot symbolize the three forefathers, Abraham, Isaac and Jacob, and also the three measures of white flour from which Abraham commanded Sarah to bake matzot for the three angels who unexpectedly honoured them with their visit.

In front of each person is a wine cup – the best you have – which is filled four times during the course of the meal. Four cups of wine symbolize the four stages of our deliverance as described in the second Book of Moses: "I will bring you out from

Passover Haggadah, The song "Lamb, oh lamb" I, II, Moravia, 1728

under the burdens of the Egyptians, and I will rid you out of their bondage, and I will redeem you with a stretched out arm, and with great judgements: And I will take you to me for a people, and I will be to you a God" (Ex. Chap. 6:6–8). According to Rabbi Loew, the four kingdoms which ruled Israel after Egypt were Babylon, Persia, Greece and Rome. The famous Rabbi Loew joins them with Sarah, Rivka, Rachel and Leah whose virtues and credits contributed to the future deliverance of the Israelites from Egypt. We give preference to red wine which recalls the blood of circumcision as the foundation stone of the Covenant which the Lord and the Israelites concluded on Mount Sinai, as well as the blood of the Passover sacrifice which the Israelites spread on their doorframes to save their firstborn from the tenth Egyptian plague. However, the cup of wine is not just reserved for those at the meal; the largest one is set aside on the table for the Prophet Elijah, who is symbolically welcomed to the seder table as the most honoured guest. The Prophet Elijah, who announced the coming of the Messiah, clearly shows a further dimension to the seder service, which is not only a memory of past deliverance, but also a promise of future salvation.

The seder meal does not just consist of food and drink. "It is our obligation to talk about the deliverance from Egypt because he who talks at greater length about deliverance from Egypt, then he deserves praise," we read in the Haggadah, a slim but very rich and wise book, full of beautiful stories and pictures. Apparently it is the oldest used ritual text and one of only a few prayer books which contain rich illustrations. The word *Haggadah* in Hebrew means "telling a story". The main point of the *Haggadah* is the story of the biblical tale about the Exodus from Egypt, richly developed and completed with the passages from the Torah and commentaries taken from the *Midrash*. It contains many prayers, blessings, psalms and interpretations of individual ritual acts which it records in precise order. The Haggadah ends with the traditional seder song about the lamb so eagerly awaited by all the children in the family. At the end of the *Haggadah*, the counting of the omer is added, which begins after the second day of Passover.

The *Haggadah* is an integral part of the seder. The father reads from it, but usually everyone has a copy in front of them on the table so that they can follow the text and not miss anything of importance. Those who cannot read yet listen carefully to the words of the *Haggadah*. Everything which takes place during the seder meal aims to awaken the curiosity of the children and force them to ask questions about the meaning of biblical events. This fulfils the commandment of the Lord: "And it shall be when thy son asketh thee in time to come, saying, What is this? that thou shalt say unto him, by strength of hand the Lord brought us out from Egypt, from the house of bondage" (Ex. Chap. 13:14). It is no coincidence that the youngest member of the family reads from the passage beginning with the following words: *"Ma nishtane ha laila ha zeh?"* (Why is this night different from all other nights?)

Passover Haggadah, the preparation of the seder, Moravia, 1728

Passover Haggadah, in a windmill, Germany, 1460–1470

First Mother fattened up a drake so the fat would be *Yontovdik*. Father ordered 12–15 kilograms of matzot so there would be enough to hand round. Mother put aside a large basket of eggs and was greatly encouraged by the hens. A week before the festival everything was cleaned, whitewashed and scrubbed. We could hardly wait to get home from school and be able to help take down carefully the festive pots and utensils from the attic.

Mother had her hands full of work in the kitchen. We could help with the salting and cutting of the goose fat. Once the hotplate, oven, mortar and the bench around the hotplate were made up with red-hot coal and pebbles, and the *chometz*, i.e. the leaven, was burnt, Mother had only the seder dishes left to prepare. She baked the eggs in the ash and boiled the bone in salted water, prepared the parsley and horseradish, grated the apple, added the chopped almonds and placed each dish on a separate plate. She then took an extra long towel and always folded it over a flawless whole matzah three times so they lay

one on top of another. It was not always so easy to find one without any flaws. On top she placed a cover with embroidered Hebrew letters and on top of this all the small bowls with the eggs and bones in the middle. When preparing for these feasts Mother's pleasant and beautiful face would express a special festive joy which was transferred to us her six children when we came home, and we would crowd round her, following all her actions with sacred respect. Finally everything was ready, even the popular dumplings for the soup which I was allowed to make with my elder sister. We then ran to the garden to pick some violets to place in the vase between the candlesticks. Mother lit a candle, lifted up her arms and said *broche*. Father opened a bottle of wine, poured everyone a small cup, handed out the Haggadahs and the whole family sat down at the table after washing their hands. The youngest sister said *ma nishtana*, Father led with the individual *broche* and we repeated them. Of course we could far from cope with the readings from the Haggadah, but we did manage to hold our own by emptying the cups of wine (we, the children, had ours diluted with water). Father would greatly improve the flavour of the bitter herbs with apple and sweetened it with a smile, but some were, after all, found under the table. But we did keep up when having to lean to the left and right sides of the table and conscientiously counted the ten Egyptian plagues with the ten touches of the little finger on the edge of the cup. Father's praying was beautiful and melodious, but we were sorry we could not really understand it. We were restless and would whisper to each other which resulted in a strict and scalding look from our Father. We were happy when the evening meal was served and we no longer had to stay quiet.

The next morning we looked forward to coffee and matzot.

We broke the matzot into considerably larger mugs and then Mother would pour hot coffee into them. In the morning we also had fried egg on matzot or hard-boiled eggs in abundance. For lunch we got *matzeloksh* with wine mousse, and meat with apple horseradish or a fruit salad made of prunes and apples. For the other days, besides potatoes we had plum scones, *grimslech*, some pudding with wine mousse and *matzeloksh* again. However, our favourite were *magronky* which mother knew how to make very well.

These were the most beautiful of family feasts and we enjoy recalling these times and regret that we will never be able to celebrate them in such a way again.

VALENTINA TURNOVSKÁ, died in Auschwitz 1942–43 (unpublished)

Several days before the festival of Passover a poor man somewhere in Russia came to the Rabbi for advice. He complained bitterly: "I've found myself in a terrible situation. The feast of Passover is almost here and I have no means to celebrate it. I have no money for matzot or meat, let alone for any festive wine. I and my family cannot show ourselves at the synagogue for the festival services. We all have only old and worn clothes." The Rabbi tried to comfort him with the words: "Don't worry. The Almighty shall help you." However, he could not calm the unhappy man. "I have so many worries, Rabbi," he complained. "It is all too much for me." – "Well," said the Rabbi,

"if that is the case then we'll have a look at them together." And immediately he began to count. "How much do you need for matzot, meat and festive wine?" – "Sixteen roubles." – "And to clothe your children?" – "Eighteen roubles." – "And for new clothes for your wife?" – "Eight roubles." – "And for a new suit for yourself?" – "Ten roubles."

The Rabbi sat at his table, counted everything up and said: "You need fifty-two roubles altogether. So you see, you no longer have to worry about how to obtain the matzot, meat, festive wine and clothes for the whole family. You only have one problem now – how to acquire fifty-two roubles!"

NATHAN AUSUBEL, *Only One Problem, "A Treasury of Jewish Folklore"*

When Rabbi Baruch had burned all that was leavened on the eve of Passover and had scattered the ash, he uttered the prescribed phrase and explained it as follows: "All that is leavened which is at my reach – all the moroseness within me – all that I have and have not seen – although I think I did look

after my soul, I must, of course, have not looked after it perfectly – what I burned and did not burn – an evil instinct wants to lead me to believe that I burned everything, but I now see that I did not burn the evil instinct itself: therefore I ask you, God, let it be destroyed and trampled on as the dust of the earth."

MARTIN BUBER, *Hasidic Tales*

It was not enough getting rid of everything that was leavened, it also had to be expressed visually. This was done in the following way: on the evening before, *erev Passover*, the man and woman of the household would go through the entire house so the man of the house, responsible for all before the Lord, could remove all that was leavened. For this purpose she would cut several pieces of bread and lay them on a table, a bench, a window in a room and in several places in the kitchen. The man of the house would hold a wide cooking spoon in one hand and a lighted candle and feather duster in the other. The woman would lead him to all the places where she had put the bread, he would sweep them onto the cooking spoon and hold the light of the candle up to all the corners to make sure that no piece of *chametz* had been left behind. At the start of this ritual he would say a blessing and after the search a declaration annulling the *chametz* that had not been found. He could not say a word during the ritual for fear of desecrating it. The children would use this for their childish jokes. They too would hide *chametz* in various places and force Father to follow them up into the attic, down into the cellar, out into the shed and Father had

to follow them in silence, and whenever he found something leavened, the chilren would express their joy in noisy laughter. On *erev Passover*, first thing in the morning, the shammes would cry out in the street that the time had come to burn the *chametz*. Women from all households or cooks would come out of all the houses bringing bags with a cooking spoon, feather duster, candle and the pieces of gathered bread and hand them over to him together with several eggs.

When the shammes had collected all the *chametz* from the whole street, he would go home. There he was awaited by many boys who would take the burden from him. They would take it out of the town where they would make up a fire and burn everything – the cooking spoons, feather duster, candles and pieces of bread. During this the shammes would utter the prescribed prayers. At ten o'clock in the morning the shammes went along the street and declared that all that was leavened had been burnt and that from that moment right to the end of the feast, nothing leavened could be eaten. At that moment a festive glitter would enter the Jewish houses and Jewish streets.

LEOPOLD KOMPERT, *Aus dem Ghetto*

The mill in which the holy flour was milled had to be cleaned from the roof timbers right down to the ground and even the furthest corners had to be swept out and not a grain from the previously milled flour could be left behind. And the problems caused by the mill lads hired to help prepare the holy flour! The miller kept having to run after them and call out: "My good folk, be careful and don't eat any of the bread here!" And he had to look at their fingers so none of the flour would disappear. Why was a rich miller to eat Jewish festive flour? Why sell it? Why should he feed it to his poultry?

Finally the milling was completed and the flour was poured into new bags, transported to the town and stored in empty rooms whose walls were freshly whitewashed and the floor was scrubbed clean. The *shammes* declared in the synagogue and on the street that the flour could be obtained at such and such a place.

After that everyone hurried to pay for their portion of festive flour. Of course the husband and wife would confer before the purchase was carried out. A year always saw changes in a family. The children had grown and so had their stomachs. Sometimes a family was expecting guests and did not know how many of them would come. Of course, Mother would have liked to economize and purchase as little as possible as each pound cost a lot of money. But Father wanted the children to eat their fill. After long discussions and quarrels they finally decided on a figure which would suit both.

What did the festival bakery look like at this time? Whoever went in was welcomed with a cry and noise as many people were employed there in the preparation of unleavened bread. They stood at long tables plated with polished copper. Their hands all moved in one rhythm, one had a piece of dough before him and with a rolling pin rolled it out into a round flat shape. Then he moved the dough on to the next person who would prick it all over with sharp sticks so the heat of the fire could penetrate from all the sides of the dough and prevent it from fermenting. The pricked dough would be placed on a stick carried by a boy who would hurry over to an skilful baker who would immediately place it in the hot oven.

The entire production rested mainly on three people. The first weighed, the second kneaded and the third placed the dough in the oven. This trio were worthy of admiration and sympathy at the same time. Theirs was the most demanding work. The first weighed the flour and portioned it out to the kneader who mixed it up and quickly kneaded it in a small copper boiling pot, so he had to be highly dexterous so the dough would not begin to ferment and rise. So many a distrustful gaze followed his work. The person placing the bread in the oven was, of course, the baker himself. The baker placed the thoroughly kneaded dough, pricked with sharp sticks, on a shovel and skilfully placed it in the oven. It was baked in a couple of minutes. The housewife would then place the baked matzah on the table covered with a white tablecloth.

There was one more figure who walked in among this throng. This was the rabbi, or his substitute, who would make sure that all the rules about religion, cleanliness and order would be observed. He supervised the kneader and the baker and all those employed, making sure nothing occurred which would breach the rules. Questions requiring a religious ruling were also put to him, which he was obliged to resolve immediately. For example, some matzot had not been pricked properly and, when they were placed in the oven, they would swell up. The devout housewife was at a loss and so she would submit them to the supervisor for examination. He would decide whether or not they were suitable for the feasts. If not, then they became a welcome quarry for the children who plunged at them like hungry wolves.

The greatest care was devoted to the so-called "mitzvah" matzot for both seders during which the whole family recalled the departure of their ancestors from Egypt. They used to be a little larger than normal matzot, and nicer.

Once the work was done, the employees received their remuneration, they were not satisfied, however, if they did not receive the agreed wage and a good tip.

Mention must be made of the respect shown during the baking of the matzot for the rabbi for whom matzot were not baked until the last day. Where there was a Talmud school or "Yeshiva", the pupils would themselves bake matzot for the rabbi for whom this had three advantages: 1. He received completely fresh matzot, 2. They were completely flawless, 3. The matzot were completely clean. Many a Jew wished for such advantages, not to mention others, so his son could become a rabbi.

LEOPOLD KOMPERT, *Aus dem Ghetto*

CHAROSET

Ashkenazi charoset

3 apples, peeled and
  grated
1 cup/5½ oz blanched,
  chopped almonds
1 cup/8 oz chopped
  raisins
1–2 tsp ground cinnamon
1 tbsp sweet red Passover
  wine

Mix the apples with the
almonds, raisins and
cinnamon, and add the wine.
Mix everything together to
form a crunchy paste.

Sephardi charoset

2 cups/1 lb pitted dates
2 cups/1 lb raisins
2 cups/16 fl oz water
½ cup/2 oz ground
  almonds or walnuts
1 tsp ground
  cinnamon
2–4 tbsp sweet red
  Passover wine

Leave the dates and raisins to soak for 1 hour in the water in a pan. Bring to the
boil and simmer for 30–60 minutes. Crush or blend them and leave to cool. Add
the almonds or walnuts, the cinnamon and the wine, and mix together well.
There are other variations on charoset such as those including oranges, figs,
dried apricots, or bananas thickened with matzah meal.

BORSCH (WITH MEAT)

Serves 10

$2\frac{1}{4}$ lb prime beef
15 cups/6 pints water
6 medium-sized
  beetroots, grated
2 onions, finely chopped
2 cloves garlic, crushed
1 tbsp salt
3 tsp sugar
5 tsp lemon juice
2 eggs

Place the meat in a large saucepan, cover with water and bring to the boil. Allow to boil for a little while and then skim off the froth. Add the beetroot, onion, garlic and salt, cover and cook for approximately 2 hours until the meat is tender. Add the sugar and lemon juice and cook for another 15 minutes. Remove 2 cups/16 fl oz of the soup, allow to cool and then beat in the eggs. Return to the soup and cook for another 10–15 minutes. Serve the soup warm with pieces of the meat.

MATZAH DUMPLINGS

Serves 4

2 eggs, separated
3 tbsp chicken fat, gently heated
½ cup/4 fl oz boiling chicken stock
1 cup/8 oz matzah meal
1 tsp salt
1 tsp ground ginger

Mix the egg yolks with the chicken fat and stock. Combine the matzah meal, salt and ginger in a bowl, and pour in the egg-yolk mixture. Mix well. Beat the egg whites until they are stiff and form peaks. Fold into the dumpling mixture and chill for 1 hour.
Using wet hands, form the mixture into round walnut-sized dumplings. Bring a large pan of salted water to the boil, add the dumplings, cover and cook for 25 minutes. Drain and serve in chicken or beef soup. They can also be served as a side dish.

ALMOND DUMPLINGS

Serves 4

2 eggs, separated
1 cup/5½ oz blanched, chopped almonds
½ tsp salt
oil for frying

Beat the egg yolks and stir in the almonds and salt. Beat the egg whites until stiff and forming peaks. Fold into the egg and nut mixture. Heat the oil and add teaspoons of the dumpling mixture, frying until brown. Serve with beef or chicken soup.

MATZOT BAKED WITH SPINACH AND MEAT

Serves 4

6 tbsp vegetable oil
1 medium-sized onion, finely chopped
$10\frac{1}{2}$ oz ground beef
1 tsp salt
$1\frac{1}{4}$ lb frozen spinach
1 cup/8 oz mashed potato
3 eggs
3 matzot

To prepare the filling

Heat 2 tablespoons of the oil in a pan and fry the onion until browned. Add the beef and the salt and fry until the meat is brown. Mix in the frozen spinach, mashed potatoes and two of the eggs, beaten first. Mix well. Preheat the oven to 350°F/Gas 4. Soak the matzot in cold water for approximately 2 minutes. When they are soft, remove from the water and dry on kitchen paper. Grease a roasting pan with 2 tablespoons of oil, place two matzot one on top of the other and spread the filling on top. Then place the third matzah on top of that. Beat the remaining egg, and pour over the matzah together with the remaining oil. Bake for 20–30 minutes.

BAKED CHEESE AND MATZOT

Serves 4 to 5

4 cups/8½ oz grated hard cheese such as Cheddar

4 cups/8½ oz grated white salted cheese

6 matzot

2 tbsp olive oil, plus extra for greasing

Preheat the oven to 350°F/Gas 4. Mix the cheeses together. Pour hot water over the matzot, leave to soak for about 1 minute and then drain when they are soft. Layer the matzot with the mixture of grated cheeses in a greased ovenproof dish. Sprinkle each layer with the olive oil. The final layer should be of matzah. Bake for 15–20 minutes until the top is lightly browned.

MATZAH PUDDING

Serves 4

5 matzot
2 tbsp vegetable oil or
  poultry fat, plus extra
  for greasing
3 eggs, beaten
2 tbsp gribenes (see
  below)
1 tsp salt
$\frac{1}{4}$ tsp ground black pepper
2 tsp sugar

Preheat the oven to
350°F/Gas 4. Soak the
matzot in cold water for
about 1 minute. When
soft, squeeze gently to
remove the water. Mix
with the oil or fat. Add
the eggs, gribenes, salt,
pepper and sugar. Bake in
a well-greased ovenproof
dish for approximately 45
minutes. Serve warm as a
side dish to accompany
meat.

GRIBENES

2 cups/4 oz fat and skin
  from the back of a hen,
  duck or goose
1 onion, sliced into rings

Cut the fat and skin into small pieces and fry gently on a low heat for 3 minutes.
Add the onion and continue frying until the fat melts and the onion and skin are
browned. Pour away the fat and store the gribenes in a refrigerator.

MATZAH KUGEL WITH SMOKED MEAT

Serves 5 to 7

$1\frac{1}{4}$ lb smoked beef, finely
   chopped
6 eggs, separated
$\frac{1}{2}$ cup/4 fl oz stock
1 cup/4 oz matzah meal
$\frac{1}{2}$ tsp salt
$\frac{1}{2}$ tsp ground black pepper
large bunch fresh chives
   or parsley, finely
   chopped
6 egg whites, stiffly
   beaten
vegetable oil for greasing

Preheat the oven to
350°F/Gas 4. Mix the beef
with the egg yolks, add the
stock and matzah meal,
salt, pepper and chives or
parsley. Beat the egg
whites until stiff and
forming peaks and fold
into the meat mixture.
Put into a greased oven-
proof dish and bake for
approximately 45 minutes.

LITVAK MATZAH KUGEL

(Illustrated left)

Serves 6 to 8

9 eggs
$\frac{1}{2}$ tsp salt
2 tbsp chicken fat or
   margarine, plus extra
   for greasing
3 cups/12 oz matzah meal
2 cups/16 fl oz water
2 cups/$3\frac{1}{2}$ oz cooked
   ground beef or chicken
1 onion, finely chopped or
   2 tbsp gribenes (see
   page 161)
$\frac{1}{2}$ tsp ground black pepper
1 tsp ground ginger

Whisk the eggs well and mix with the salt and chicken fat or margarine. Add the matzah meal and the water gradually until the dough is the consistency of fresh, raw pasta. Chill for 1 hour, then roll out. Meanwhile mix the meat with the onion or gribenes, add the pepper and ginger. Preheat the oven to 350°F/Gas 4. Press part of pastry on the bottom of a greased roasting pan, then spoon and spread alternate layers of the meat and pastry mixtures. The final layer should be of pastry. Bake for 1 hour. Serve the kugel in slices with beef or chicken soup.

STEWED CHICKEN WITH PRUNES

Serves 4

2 tbsp vegetable oil
1 medium-sized onion,
   finely chopped
$3\frac{1}{2}$ lb chicken, cut into
   portions
3 tbsp ground cinnamon
1 tbsp ground ginger
$\frac{1}{2}$ tbsp ground black
   pepper
1 tsp salt
1 cup/8 fl oz water
2 cups/1 lb pitted prunes,
   soaked overnight
1 tbsp demerara sugar or
   honey
$\frac{1}{2}$ cup/$2\frac{1}{2}$ oz whole
   blanched almonds

Heat the oil, add the onion and fry until lightly browned. Push it to the sides of the pan and lightly brown the portions of chicken on all sides. Sprinkle the cinnamon, ginger, pepper and salt over the chicken and add the water. Bring to the boil, cover and simmer for approximately 30 minutes, stirring occasionally. Put the prunes and their soaking water around the chicken, add the sugar or honey, cover again and continue to simmer for another 20 minutes or so until the chicken is tender. If necessary, add more water during the cooking time. Lightly roast the almonds in the oven and add to the sauce. To serve pour the sauce over the chicken in a serving dish.

MATZAH AND COTTAGE CHEESE BALLS

Serves 3

1 cup/4 oz cottage cheese
$\frac{1}{2}$ cup/2 oz matzah meal
1 egg, beaten
$\frac{1}{2}$ tsp salt
$\frac{1}{8}$ tsp ground black pepper
matzah meal for coating
oil for frying
light (single) cream, to
  serve

Mix the cottage cheese with the matzah meal, stir in the egg, add the salt and pepper, and using damp hands, form walnut-sized balls. Coat in the matzah meal. Heat the oil and fry until golden. Serve with the cream.

EGGS WITH MATZOT

Serves 2

3 matzot
2 tsp grated onion
3 eggs, beaten
½ tsp salt
butter or other fat for
    frying

Soak the matzot briefly in cold water until soft, then drain and squeeze out the water. Mix with the onion, eggs and salt. Leave to rest for 15 minutes. Heat the butter or fat and fry the mixture on both sides until golden.
Cut into portions and serve immediately.

POTATO KUGEL

(Illustrated left)

Serves 4

6 medium-sized potatoes,
    peeled and grated
1 onion, grated
½ cup/2 oz matzah meal
2 eggs, beaten
7 tbsp vegetable oil, plus
    extra for greasing
¾ tbsp salt

Preheat the oven to 350°F/Gas 4. Mix the grated potatoes with the onion, add the matzah meal, eggs, oil and salt and stir well. Grease an ovenproof dish, and place in the oven for 5 minutes. Put the kugel mixture into the hot dish and bake for about 45 minutes until brown and crispy on top.

MATZAH MEAL PANCAKES WITH CINNAMON

Serves 4

3 eggs
1 cup/8 fl oz milk or
  water

1 cup/4 oz matzah
  meal
$\frac{1}{2}$ tsp salt
1 tsp sugar
oil for frying
ground cinnamon
  mixed with sugar for
  dusting

Beat the eggs with the water or milk. Add the matzah meal and stir well. Add the salt and sugar. Heat the oil and add tablespoons of the mixture to the pan, frying on both sides until golden. Dust with the cinnamon while still hot and serve immediately.

PESACH BLINTZES

(Illustrated right)

Makes approximately 20 blintzes

For the batter

6 eggs
1 cup/4 oz potato flour
2 cups/16 fl oz water
4 tbsp vegetable oil, plus
  extra for greasing

For the sweet fillings

For the cottage cheese filling

2 cups/8 oz cottage
  cheese
2 tbsp sugar
1 egg yolk
$\frac{1}{2}$ tsp vanilla extract
  (essence)
$\frac{1}{2}$ cup milk
$\frac{1}{2}$ cup/4 oz raisins

Cream the cottage cheese with the sugar and egg yolk, flavour with the vanilla extract (essence) and pour in the milk. Finally mix in the raisins.

For the apple filling

$2\frac{1}{4}$ lb peeled and cubed
  apples
1 tsp ground
  cinnamon
$\frac{1}{4}$ cup/2 oz sugar
$\frac{1}{4}$ cup/$1\frac{1}{2}$ oz chopped
  walnuts
$\frac{1}{2}$ cup/4 oz raisins
1 tsp lemon juice
Combine all the
ingredients in a large
bowl and mix well.

For the savoury fillings

For the mushroom filling

1¼ lb mushrooms
½ tsp salt
¼ tsp ground black pepper
1 tbsp butter
2 eggs, beaten

Chop the mushrooms and add the salt and pepper. Heat the butter until melted and gently fry the mushrooms until soft. Add the eggs, stir gently and allow to cook for a minute until the egg sets.

For the spinach filling

1 tbsp butter or margarine
1 onion, finely chopped
1 tsp matzah meal
8½ oz frozen spinach
½ tsp salt
¼ tsp ground black pepper
pinch of grated nutmeg
¼ cup/2 fl oz milk
1 egg, beaten

Heat the butter or margarine until melted. Add the onion and fry until lightly browned. Sprinkle over the matzah meal and stir in. Add the frozen spinach, salt, pepper and nutmeg. Cook for about 10 minutes until the spinach has defrosted, pour in the milk and then add the egg and cook for a couple of minutes longer. As a variation, 2 crushed cloves of garlic may be added after the onion has

been fried. To prepare the blintzes, beat the eggs until frothy and gradually add the potato flour and water. Continue whisking for approximately 5 minutes until the batter is very light and frothy. Heat a small amount of oil in a pan and using a ladle, pour in a very thin layer of batter so it covers the whole pan. Fry until golden yellow. Place the cooked blintzes on top of each other on a warmed plate. Preheat the oven to 350°F/Gas 4. Place a heaped tablespoon of filling in the centre of each blintz and roll up. Place in a greased roasting pan, lightly coat with oil and bake until golden, approximately 20 minutes. Serve blintzes with a sweet filling with cream, and the savoury ones with cabbage.

MATZAH KRINZEL

Makes 15 to 20

3 matzot
2 eggs, separated
$\frac{1}{4}$ tsp salt
$\frac{1}{4}$ tsp ground cinnamon
3 tsp sugar
1 tbsp ground almonds
1 tbsp lemon juice
1 cup/8 oz chopped
  raisins
oil for frying
confectioner's (icing)
  sugar for dusting

Soak the matzot in cold water until soft. Drain and squeeze out the water. Mix them with the egg yolks. Beat in the salt, cinnamon, sugar, almonds, lemon juice and raisins. Beat the egg whites until siff and forming peaks. Fold into the matzah mixture. Heat the oil and add tablespoons of the mixture, frying on both sides until golden. Dust with confectioner's (icing) sugar and serve with stewed prunes and orange.

ALMOND SWEETMEATS

Makes approximately 30

1 cup/4 oz ground
  almonds
2 cups/10 oz
  confectioner's (icing)
  sugar
1 tbsp ground cinnamon
1 tbsp fine matzah meal
3 egg whites
margarine for greasing

Preheat the oven to 250°F/Gas 1–2. Mix the almonds, sugar, cinnamon and matzah meal together. Beat the egg whites until stiff and forming peaks. Fold into the almond mixture. If the mixture is too thin, add some more matzah meal. With wet hands, form balls about 1 in in diameter and place them, well spaced, on a greased baking tray. Bake for approximately 25 minutes until firm.

DESSERT TZIMMES

Serves 6 to 8

3 cups/1½ lb prunes
2 cups/1 lb dried apricots
2 cups/1 lb dried pears
1 cup/8 oz dried apples

½ tsp ground
  cinnamon
1 tsp sugar

Wash the dried fruit in hot water, cut up the larger pears, place in a pan with the cinnamon and sugar, cover with boiling water and cook until the fruit is tender, about 30 minutes. Leave to cool at room temperature, and serve.

PESACH SPONGE

(Illustrated left)

Serves 6 to 8

6 eggs, separated
1 cup/8 oz sugar
juice of 1 lemon
1 cup/4 oz matzah meal,
  sifted
4 tbsp potato flour
¼ tsp salt
margarine for greasing

For the icing

2 cups/10 oz
  confectioner's (icing)
  sugar
1 cup/8 fl oz water
juice of 1 lemon
½ tsp vanilla extract
  (essence)
2 egg whites

Preheat the oven to 325°F/Gas 3. To make the sponge, cream the egg yolks with the sugar until they turn pale yellow, add the lemon juice and the matzah meal mixed with the potato flour and salt. Beat the egg whites until they are stiff and form peaks. Fold in to the sponge mixture. Bake in a greased cake pan (tin) for approximately 45 minutes until firm to the touch. Leave to cool. To prepare the icing, boil the sugar with the water for 5 minutes, add the lemon juice and the vanilla extract (essence) and leave to cool. Beat the egg whites until stiff and forming peaks. Fold in to the icing syrup. Ice the cake or cover it with whipped cream and fruit.

MATZAH ALMOND GÂTEAU

(Illustrated right)

Serves 8

8 eggs, separated
1½ cups/12 oz sugar
¼ cup/1 oz matzah meal, sifted, plus extra for dusting
½ tbsp lemon juice
¾ tsp salt
1 tbsp cold water
½ cup/2 oz ground walnuts
½ cup/2 oz ground almonds
margarine for greasing

Preheat the oven to 350°F/Gas 4. Beat the egg yolks until light and frothy and gradually add the sugar. When the yolks turn pale yellow, add the matzah meal, lemon juice, salt and water. Stir in the walnuts and almonds. Beat the egg whites until stiff and forming peaks. Fold into the cake mixture. Turn the mixture into a greased and dusted cake pan (tin). Bake for approximately 45 minutes until firm to the touch.

For the icing

1 egg yolk
½ cup/4 fl oz lemon juice
½ cup/4 oz sugar
1 tbsp margarine

Gently heat the egg yolk, sugar and lemon juice over a low heat in a pan, stirring constantly. When the mixture has thickened, remove from the heat. Add the margarine and stir well. Ice the cake when cooled but still in the pan (tin). When the icing has set, remove from the tin.

MATZAH KUGEL WITH WINE

Serves 4

4 matzot
1½ cups/12 fl oz wine
1 cup/8 oz raisins
1 cup/5½ oz walnuts, finely chopped
1 cup/8 oz sugar
2 tsp cinnamon
3 egg whites, beaten until stiff
margarine for greasing

Leave the matzot to soak in half the wine until soft, adding a little water if necessary to make sure they are moist. Mix together the raisins, chopped walnuts, sugar and cinnamon. Stir in the stiffly beaten egg whites. Grease the dish well with margarine and fill it with alternate layers of matzah and nut raisin mixture. The top layer should be matzah. Bake at 350°F/Gas 4 for approximately 35 minutes, then pour on the remaining wine and bake for another 5 minutes.

SHAVUOT
חג השבועות

"Seven weeks shalt thou number unto thee; begin to number the seven weeks from such a time as thou beginnest to put the sickle to the corn. And thou shalt keep the feast of weeks unto the Lord thy God with a tribute of a free will offering of thine hand, which thou shalt give unto the Lord thy God, according as the Lord thy God hath blessed thee" (Deut. Chap. 16:9–10).

With these words the Torah commands all the people of Israel to celebrate Shavuot, the Feast of Weeks. Seven weeks have passed from the day when the first sheaves of barley were laid on the Lord's altar, the time has come for the new harvest. *Chag ha-katzir*, the harvest festival, is celebrated on the 6th of Sivan. Crowds of pilgrims flood into the Holy City from early morning to lay on the Lord's altar freshly baked bread made from the first harvest of wheat and *bikkurim* – the best crop from the fruit harvest. The festive processions would wind their way towards the gates of Jerusalem like a long colourful snake. Dates, figs, oranges and olives are heaped in neat piles in richly decorated baskets, crispy loaves of wheat bread are set on golden platters. The inhabitants of Jerusalem come out to meet the pilgrims and to welcome them to the Holy Temple. Everyone dances and sings; music and the joyful peal of bells are heard all around...

This atmosphere of festive pilgrimage continues in many places even today. In Israel, Shavuot is marked by grand harvest festivals, the most famous of which takes place in Haifa. Crowds of children flood the streets of the city dressed in special white robes wearing wreaths and holding green twigs in their hands. Bright banners and colourful ribbons hang on the houses. Farmers from the kibbutz carry baskets piled high with fruit and vegetables of such great variety as could only be dreamed of by their biblical ancestors.

Today, however, this feast has a different significance from the one it had at the time of the Holy Temple. According to Talmudic tradition, the 6th of Sivan is the anniversary of the Lord's appearance on Mount Sinai. In the month of Nisan the Jews were led out of Egypt and 49 days later Moses received the Ten Commandments. Forty-nine days of Omer between the feast of Passover and Shavuot is also the period which joins together two of the most important milestones in Jewish history: deliverance from Egyptian slavery and its spiritual culmination through the acceptance of the Torah. Fifty days pass before fruit appears following the blossoming apple tree, and the people of Israel waited fifty days in the wilderness before receiving the Torah from the hand of the Lord as is written in the commentary *Psikta Zutrata*. Shavuot is also *zman matan toratenu* – the time of the giving of the Torah.

The festive rituals of Shavuot celebrate the greatness of God and His holy teachings; they symbolize the events accompanying the acceptance of the Torah on Sinai. On the first night of the festival devout Jews stay awake to purify and elevate their soul as did their ancestors in the wilderness; they read selected passages from the Torah, Talmudic and cabbalistic scriptures contained in the collection *Tikun leyl Shavuot* ("Readings for the Night of Shavuot") and meditate over them. Part of the service for both days of the festival is the reading from the second book of Moses. The majestic melody of the Ten Commandments can be heard throughout the synagogue.

Left:
The Torah cloak

The Torah scroll

Ashkenazi Jews begin the reading with the liturgical poem *akdamot* from the Torah. Each of its 90 verses ends with the syllable "ta". This special form of composition is not, however, just a formal play on words: it contains a highly profound and wise message. The last and first letters of the Hebrew alphabet symbolize the end and beginning of the Torah. The Torah must be read several times. Having read right to the very last letter, we must return to the beginning and read it again. The Torah is a bottomless fount of wisdom and every Jew should study it throughout his life.

"More Torah, more life. More learning, more wisdom," the wise men used to say. So, since ancient times, the festival of Shavuot has also been dedicated to study and learning. One of the most important events in the lives of Jewish children is beginning to attend cheder – religious school. On this occasion, when they read the verses of the Torah, the first in their lives, they receive special honey cakes which have verses from the Torah inscribed on them, so they may hold "one sweet memory" and "honey and milk are under thy tongue" (Song of Songs, Chap. 4:11).

It is at this time that the Book of Ruth – *Megilat Ruth* – is read. The story takes place during the harvest and it demonstrates Ruth's wisdom, humility and self-denial. In the same way these qualities are required to be able to accept the Torah on Shavuot.

"And I am come down to deliver them out of the hand of the Egyptians, and to bring them up out of that land unto a good and a large land flowing with milk and honey" (Ex. Chap. 3:8). Just as the promised land flowed with milk and honey, so the

Plate, Bohemia (Prague), late 18th century

food on our festive table – the blintzes, pancakes, kreplach, strudel, cheesecakes and milk dishes also symbolize the events on Mount Sinai. The numerical value of the Hebrew word *chalav*, i.e. milk, is 40 and Moses had to wait 40 days on Mount Sinai before receiving the Torah from the Lord. According to tradition, the Israelites ate milk dishes after receiving the Torah, perhaps because they could not clean their vessels in the wilderness to comply with the laws of kashrut which they had received together with the Torah.

At Shavuot, cakes shaped like slabs on which the Ten Commandments were inscribed are very popular. So are conical loaves which are made to look like Mount Sinai, Sephardi Jews are proud of their "seven heavens", big round cakes with seven layers recalling the seven heavens by which the Lord came down to Mount Sinai and also the seven weeks of Omer. However, meat must also form a part of the festival meal. On both feast days two main meals are served the first of which is milk and the second meat. Shavuot is in fact the extension of Passover and these two main dishes remind us of the two main dishes of Passover – the Passover lamb and the festival sacrifice *Korban chagiga*. There is also another reason for the tradition of two festive dishes: according to the Laws of kashrut, bread from the same loaf may not be eaten with milk and meat dishes. These two loaves symbolize the bread once brought from the first harvest as a sacrifice to the Lord.

Right and opposite:
*Povijan for the Torah
(detail), Moravia, 18th
century*

S havuot – the Feast of Weeks or Pentecost – when synagogues and homes are decorated with flowers and foliage
and the words "And Moses spake unto the sons of Israel about
God's feasts" are sung, is a festival which is more a gift than a
command from God as I recall. During this time we are obliged
to pray and to enjoy ourselves.

Mother's floral decorations of the pictures were somewhat
exaggerated because we only had three wall mirrors, two en-
larged photographs of our grandfathers, *mizrach* and drawn
calendars marking the anniversaries of the death of my mater-
nal and paternal grandparents.

On the Feast of Weeks – Shavuot – the ark for the Torah in the
synagogue was decorated with so many flowers that I must also
write something about the Strakonice shammes, Mr Popper, who
deserves the credit for this. Although 14 Jewish families had
gardens, the work of picking flowers for the prayerhouse was
done by the caretaker of the synagogue. Mr Popper was both the
shammes (caretaker) and *shochet* (kosher meat slaughterer),
and in view of his many functions, he was in fact the backbone
of the life of the Jewish religious community.

R. EHRMANN, *In Strakonice*

The most fundamental part of our religious education was based on strict food laws. What was and was not permitted, when one could eat meat and milk foods, how many hours had to pass before one could eat milk after meat food... There were three sets of utensils: the grandest was the *yomtordik* set for Pesach which was an ancient set and had been handed down from generation to generation. It consisted of bowls, plates, roasting pans, pots and saucepans of faded colours and strange-looking ancient shapes. They are hidden away from human eyes for the whole year as they were stored in the attic behind the chimney in an old worm-eaten box. On the eve of the festival, it was taken down with great ceremony only to be returned after the eight days of feasting to the gloom of the attic.

Then there was the ordinary set of utensils for the meat and an ordinary set for the milk food. The milk tablespoons had white laces on the handles so they could not be confused with the meat spoons which did not have these laces.

The food laws were strictly observed and our parents would always remind us, the children, that whoever sinned against any of these laws would not see the light of the next day and would most certainly die.

VOJTĚCH RAKOUS, *Modche and Rezi*

Shavuot... Work is put aside and it can be discerned from everything, objects and people, that there is a feast – the great feast. And throughout the entire cottage, in every corner there is the tingling scent of lilac ... the sweet scent of lilac.

Cakes were baked two days before the feast. On the last two weekdays these were "rohatiny" (peg boards) made of rye flour and on the feast days cakes made from the finest "vejražka" flour. The cakes were always baked in the furnace at night. All the women in the neighbourhood were asked to come and bake.

On the eve of Shavuot we, the children, would go into the neighbours' gardens to look for "greenery", lilac twigs and fresh lilac blossoms. On that day our room looked like a grove in blossom. Everywhere on the walls where there was an empty space, there were green lilac twigs and lilac flowers.

These lilac flowers were everywhere. Lilac flowers decorated the space above the door, above the mirror, between the windows and were even on the many portraits which covered the walls of the room. The faded portraits of old aunts in old-fashioned crinolines and even more old-fashioned caps appeared strange under the fresh spring decoration. The scent of lilac flowers spread throughout the whole cottage and we could breathe in this scent for two days and two nights.

The two feast days seemed like one long fairy tale. In the morning there were cakes (instead of a slice of bread) to indulge in, then the journey to synagogue through the spring crops and the sunlight, then the festive dinner at home.

VOJTĚCH RAKOUS, *Modche and Rezi*

STUFFED EGGS

Serves 3

6 hard-boiled eggs
2 tbsp finely chopped
   pickled gherkins
3 tbsp cream cheese
1 tbsp mustard
salt
ground black pepper

Cut the eggs in half and scoop out the yolks. Mix the yolks with the gherkins, cream cheese, mustard, salt and pepper to form a smooth paste. Use to fill the halved egg whites and chill for a while to firm. Serve with the dill sauce.

For the dill sauce
$\frac{1}{2}$ cup/4 oz ready-made
   mayonnaise
$\frac{1}{2}$ tbsp finely chopped
   onion
1 tbsp freshly chopped
   dill
salt

Mix the mayonnaise with the onion and dill and add the salt. Keep chilled before use.

BAGELS

Makes about 15–20

1 tsp dried yeast
1 cup/8 fl oz warm water
½ tbsp sugar
1 tbsp margarine, plus
   extra for greasing
1 cup/8 fl oz hot milk
4 cups/1 lb all-purpose
   (plain) flour, sifted
1 tsp salt
1 egg yolk beaten with
   1 tsp water
sesame seeds, poppy seeds
   or caraway seeds for
   sprinkling

Stir the yeast into the warm water and add the sugar. Leave to stand for a while in a warm place. Stir the margarine into the hot milk until it has melted. Wait until the milk has cooled and pour it into the yeast.
Mix the flour with the salt in a large bowl, make a hollow in the flour and pour in the yeast liquid. Work into a soft dough. Knead the dough on a floured board and place in a greased bowl. Cover and leave in a warm place for approximately 1 hour until the dough has risen to twice its size. Knead the dough again and cut it into pieces. Knead each piece and roll it into a rope about 6 in long. Make these into rings and press the ends firmly together. Leave for 10 minutes to rise. Preheat the oven to 350°F/Gas 4. Bring a large pan of salted water to the boil. Put one risen bagel after another into the boiling water, cover and bring back to the boil. Turn the bagels over with a slotted spoon, cover and leave to boil for approximately 3–4 minutes. Remove from the water, drain and place on a greased baking tray. Brush with the egg yolk and water mixture and sprinkle with the poppy, sesame or caraway seeds. Bake until golden, about 20 minutes. Bagels are traditionally served on Shavuot with cream cheese and smoked salmon.

BAKED RICE
WITH CHEESE

Serves 4 to 6

3 cups/6 oz finely grated
 carrots
2 cups/8 oz boiled rice
2 eggs, beaten
$\frac{1}{2}$ cup heavy (double)
 cream

$1\frac{1}{2}$ tsp salt
$\frac{1}{2}$ tsp ground black pepper
3 tsp grated onion
2 cups/$3\frac{1}{2}$ oz grated
 strong (mature) cheese
 such as Cheddar
vegetable oil for greasing

Preheat the oven to 350°F/Gas 4. Mix the carrots, rice,
eggs and cream together, add the salt, pepper, onion
and half the grated cheese. Mix well and place in a
greased ovenproof dish, sprinkle with the rest of the
cheese and bake for 50 minutes.

BAKED FISH WITH POTATOES

Serves 3 to 4

2 tbsp butter, plus extra
  for greasing
2 medium-sized onions,
  thinly sliced
8 medium-sized potatoes,
  peeled and very thinly
  sliced
$1\frac{1}{4}$ lb boiled fish (e.g. carp,
  herring, cod, hake)
1–2 tsp salt
$\frac{1}{2}$ ground black pepper
2 eggs
$1\frac{1}{2}$ cup/12 fl oz heavy
  (double) cream

Preheat the oven to 350°F/Gas 4. Heat the butter in a pan, add the onion and fry slowly until browned. Layer the onion with the potato and fish in a greased ovenproof dish. Begin and end with a layer of potatoes. Sprinkle each layer with salt and pepper. Beat the eggs with the cream and pour on top of the potatoes. Bake for 45–55 minutes until golden.

NOODLE KUGEL WITH COTTAGE CHEESE AND APPLES

Serves 6 to 8

3 eggs, separated

3 tbsp sugar

2 cups/8 oz cottage cheese

$\frac{3}{4}$–1 cup/6–8 fl oz milk

5 tbsp melted margarine or butter, plus extra for greasing

5 apples, peeled and grated

1 cup/8 oz raisins

6 prunes, chopped

14 oz thin noodles, boiled

2 tbsp ground cinnamon

6 tbsp sugar

Preheat the oven to 300°F/Gas 2. Cream the egg yolks with the sugar, then gradually mix in the cottage cheese, milk, half the melted margarine or butter, apples, raisins and prunes. Mix well and add the noodles. Beat the egg whites until stiff and forming peaks, and fold into the cheese mixture. Transfer the mixture to a greased ovenproof dish, sprinkle the surface with a thick layer of cinnamon and sugar and dot with the remaining melted margarine or butter. Bake for 30–45 minutes until golden.

CHEESECAKE

Serves 6

5 eggs, separated
1 cup/8 oz sugar
2 tbsp all-purpose (plain)
   flour
2½ cups/9 oz cottage or
   curd cheese
¾ cup/6 fl oz soured cream
1 tsp vanilla extract
   (essence)
6 tbsp raisins
butter for greasing
breadcrumbs for dusting

Preheat the oven to 350°F/Gas 4. Beat the egg yolks with the sugar until pale yellow, add the flour, cottage or curd cheese, soured cream, vanilla and raisins and continue beating for a few minutes. Beat the egg whites until stiff and forming peaks. Fold into the cheese mixture.

Grease a cake pan (tin) and dust the sides with breadcrumbs. Pour the mixture into the cake pan (tin) and bake for 45 minutes until firm. Turn off the oven and leave the cake inside to set for approximately 15 minutes.

SEUDAT MITZVAH
סעודת מצוה

The family celebrations of *Seudat mitzvah* – literally the "feasts of the commandment" – are festivities of celebration which follow all the great family occasions: after circumcision, the redemption of the first born, barmitzvah, engagements, marriages and funerals.

Birth and circumcision

A Jewish boy enters into a sacred relationship with God and his community soon after birth. "And ye shall circumcise the flesh of your foreskin; and it shall be a token of the covenant betwixt me and you. And he that is eight days old, shall be circumcised among you" (Gen. Chap. 17:11–12). Circumcision expresses the idea of subjecting the physical body to moral law and directing bodily instinct towards fulfilling the commandment for renewing life ("breed and multiply"). Circumcision *(milah)* and the observation of the Sabbath, two of the most important symbols of the covenant between God and Israel, were the first objects of attack by enemies during the time of persecution. The neglect of both the sacred commandments was an external sign of abandoning the faith.

In some eastern communities on the first Friday evening after the birth of a son, families celebrate the home feast of *shalom zachor* which is freely translated as "welcome to this world, boy". A traditional dish of chick peas commonly called "nahit",

Left:
Sheva berachot *(Seven blessings), Italy, 1470*

Right:
Cradle, Bohemia, early 19th century

Circumcision chair, Bohemia,
c. 1800

requiring lengthy preparation on the previous day, is served. The next course tends
to be a dessert, a fruit bowl and some liquor to drink to the health of the baby –
l'chayim.

   The circumcision of a newborn boy takes place on the eighth day after his birth
either at home or, more frequently, at the synagogue, with the participation of the
entire community. It requires the presence of the *minyan*: 10 adult men. As the
baby is brought in, everyone calls out the greeting *baruch haba*, "Blessed be he who
comes". The greeting also applies to the invisible guest, Elijah the Prophet. According to rabbinical tradition, Elijah, the messenger of the covenant, participates in
each act of circumcision as a witness and as protector of the boy. The circumcision
is carried out by the *mohel*, a devout man with the relevant medical and ritual knowledge. The *sandek* (godfather) receives the child from his parents and hands him over
to the *mohel*, who sometimes for a moment places him in the chair of Elijah. Then
he puts the baby back on the sandek's knees so that he holds him firmly while the
cut is made. During the ritual, the boy's father and those present say the blessing.
After dressing the wound, the mohel says the blessing over the wine, stressing the
recollection of the sanctity of the covenant. He says the final prayer in which the boy
is given his name. The prayer ends with the wish for a prosperous life: "Just as this
little one has entered the covenant, so too may he grow up to attain the Torah, marriage and good deeds."

   On the eve of the circumcision, light refreshment is served in the family circle.
After the feast of circumcision a meal is served containing a meat dish. An example

Prayers and laws for
circumcision

of such a menu would be *challah* with smoked meat or fish prepared in various ways, accompanied by salads, such as potato or egg, a large variety of cheeses and cakes and cookies. A variation might be *challah*, fish with vegetables, roast chicken or cold roast meat, potato salad and sweet kugel. No feast is prescribed following the birth of a daughter. However, the parents arrange a celebratory meal for relatives and friends in the first weeks after the birth of their daughter.

Boys receive their name during the circumcision. Girls acquire their name when it is announced publicly in synagogue. This is either on the first Sabbath after their birth when the father is called to the reading of the Torah, or when the mother makes her first visit to the synagogue after her daugther is born.

Redemption of the firstborn

The redemption of the firstborn – *pidion ha-ben* – is part of the religious obligation concerning birth. Redemption only applies to a boy born as the first child of his mother. The firstborn of Israel, redeemed from the tenth Egyptian plague, were consecrated to the service of God (Ex. Chap. 13:2, 13). After taking part in the worship of the golden calf, they lost their position in the service of the holy tabernacle of the wilderness and were replaced by the men of the tribe of Levi (Num. Chap. 8:14–19). In remembrance of the original consecration, the *bechor* (firstborn) is redeemed. The ritual takes place on the 30th day after birth. The father presents the boy to the *cohen* (a descendant of the high priest Aaron) and in answer to his question he proclaims that the wishes to redeem his son and to pay five silver shekels for him. The *cohen* then declares the redemption and blesses the boy (Gen. Chap. 48:20; Num. Chap. 6:24–26). Tall glasses of hot tea are served with wine and brandy, with honey cakes, sponge cakes and many other similar delicacies.

Barmitzvah and Batmitzrah

An important milestone in life is the reaching of adulthood. A Jewish boy is considered an adult from the age of 13, and a girl from the age of 12. The boy becomes "barmitzvah" ("son of commandments" – attainment of the age of legal responsibility) at 13. This means that he is fully responsible for his behaviour in religious life, for fulfilling all the commandments of the Torah. Up to this time his father has been responsible for him. The boy is declared barmitzvah at a celebration which takes place in the synagogue on the first Saturday after his thirteenth birthday. He is called to the reading desk – *bimah* – and reads a prescribed portion of the Torah. Sometimes he may even make a little speech that he would rehearse well beforehand. The parents frequently serve refreshments at the synagogue to all present, and then the happy occasion is celebrated with family and friends at home. The barmitzvah boy receives

Tray for Pidion ha-ben, *Bohemia, c. 1850*

many gifts, the most precious of which is a man-sized talit, a prayer shawl with tasseled fringes at its four corners, and tefilin, long straps of black leather, each with a small leather box in which there is a parchment inscribed with verses from the Torah. He is obliged to wear them for morning prayer, as the Torah states: "And you shall bind them upon your head, and they shall be frontlets between your eyes" (Dent. Chap. 6, 8). The ritual batmitzvah ("daughter of commandments" – attainment of the age of legal responsibility for girls) does not have a fully defined form but is nevertheless celebrated in many congregations.

Wedding

The sacred bond between man and woman enjoys great respect in Jewish tradition. Its ruling and celebration can be found on the first pages of the Scriptures: "And the Lord God said, It is not good that the man should be alone; I will make a fitting helper by his side... Therefore shall a man leave his father and his mother, and shall cleave unto his wife: and they shall be one flesh" (Gen. Chap. 2:18, 24). Women and marriage find praise in many parts of the Bible – *Tanach*. King Solomon says: "Whoso findeth a wife findeth a good thing, and obtaineth favour of the Lord" (Prov. Chap. 18:22). Scholars of the Talmud not only praised marriage with their proclamations. Rabbi Yehuda bar Ilai, a distinguished religious authority of his day, did not hesitate to interrupt his lecture and join with his pupils in the wedding procession of people unknown to him. The wedding, *chatuna*, is the most important day in the life of two people. Marriage relies on mutual trust and understanding. The point of the bond of marriage is also expressed by the fact that the wedding ceremony precedes the signing of the holy agreement, the *ketubah*. The *ketubah*, written in Aramaic, defines the rights and mutual commitments of the married couple. The husband above all guarantees that he shall behave with respect to his wife and shall not leave her wihout financial support. The *ketubah* also defines the material security for the wife in case of the husband's death or divorce.

In view of the fact that the *ketubah* had to be signed during the ceremony, a wedding could not take place on the Sabbath and on Holy Days. Nor could a wedding take place during a time of mourning, nor during the three weeks before the Fast of Tishah b'Av and at the time of Omer between Passover and Shavuot, with the exception of one day – Lag b'Omer. However, the days before the wedding are not just a time for obtaining the necessary material items. The bride and groom should devote time to spiritual preparation and searching their consciences. A frequent custom at this time is a visit to the ritual bath or *mikvah*. Both the bride and groom fast on the morning of the wedding day.

The wedding takes place under a *chupah*, a marriage canopy held up by four poles. The *chupah*, which symbolizes the future home of the married couple, used to be erected under an open sky in some eastern European countries. If the wedding takes place in a synagogue, the canopy is placed on the bimah. The first to step under the canopy is the groom or *chatan*, led by his friends and witnesses. Then the wedding procession of the bride enters. The bride, *kala*, is dressed in white and has a veil over her face. She follows the example of Rebecca who covered her face when Isaac came towards her (Gen. Chap. 24:65). A small home ceremony is usually connected with the placing of the veil on the bride's head in which the rabbi and the local dignitaries often take part. On being led to the *chupah* the bride then walks around the groom seven times. So begins the first part of the ceremony, the engagement or *erusin*. The groom places a ring on the bride's right index finger and utters the ancient phrase: "Behold! You are consecrated to me with this ring according to the laws of Moses and Israel." With this the engagement is recognized by a legal mandatory act.

The second part of the ceremony is the actual wedding or *nisuin* which is preceded by the public reading of the *ketuba*. During the *nisuin* the couple each drink from the same cup of wine. During the ceremony, the *chazan* sings seven blessings. Apart from prayers for the couple's prosperity, the main theme of the ceremony is the glorification of God for creating man in his own image and the wish for the return of the voice of joy to the towns of Judea and the streets of Jerusalem. At the end of the ceremony, the groom stamps on a glass and breaks it, whereupon the wedding guests reply with the cry of *mazal tov*! – "Good luck!" The shattering of the glass fulfils the warning of the rabbis for man not to forget about the destruction of the Temple even during the happiest moments of life.

The newly married couple is allowed a short time together in private, and then the reception follows, often accompanied by dancing. The wedding reception abounds in everything that the family can afford. However, there must always be a large *challah* and the Kiddush blessing is made over it. Traditionally the groom gives a sermon, or *derasha*, on various themes taken from the Scriptures and the Talmud.

The law of Jewish marriage also concerns the so called levirate marriage, *yibum* in Hebrew. This meant that if the husband died after a childless marriage, his brother was obliged to marry the widow and the firstborn son of this marriage bore the name of the deceased. If the brother refused to marry he had to undergo a ceremony called *chalitza*, during which the brother's widow took off her shoes in front of witnesses. By this act both the widow and the late husband's brother were released from the obligation to marry.

Jewish religion allows divorce. However, a rabbinical court only gives its consent in exceptional cases when all attempts at reconciliation fail.

When the young couple moves to the new home, one of their first religious obligations is to fasten a *mezuzah*, or small case containing part of the Torah, to their doorpost. This takes place in the presence of the *minyan* during a ceremony called *chanukat ha'bayit* ("consecration of the home").

Death

During illness and in death man must not be abandoned by the Jewish community. Members of the *chevrah kaddisha* (holy group) take care of one's spiritual needs. They regularly visit a dying patient, find out about his needs and pray for him. (The group consists of men, in the case of a male, women for a female.)

After death, they light a candle at the head, stay beside the body all the time and make the funeral arrangements. The members of this devout association also give their condolences to the bereaved and try to help with problems connected with the

Group jug, Moravia, mid-19th century

Above:
Funeral group jug,
Bohemia (Prague), 1799

Above right:
Group jug, Moravia, 1836

funeral. They also perform the ritual purification (*tahara*) before the funeral. Afterwards the deceased is taken to the cemetery – *beit ha'kvarot*. The body is washed with water mixed with an egg, the symbol of life. It is dressed in a shirt, underpants and a *kittel* (shroud) with a collar. A cap is placed on the head. All parts of the clothing are white. Men are dressed in the *talit* with the decoration removed. No flowers or jewellery may be placed in the coffin which is made of unplaned boards. Jewish burial customs are characteristic in their simplicity and lack of distinction between the rich and the poor. The funeral takes place in accordance with the biblical words "Dust you are and to dust you shall return to earth."

After the prayer "What the Almighty does is perfect", and the rabbi's burial speech, the coffin is carried in a procession to the grave. It is the custom to give charitable donations to the *chevrah kaddisha*. After the coffin is lowered into the grave and after the rabbi's prayer, everyone present throws three shovels of earth onto the coffin. The funeral ends in the funeral hall with the *Kaddish* prayer and condolences to the bereaved.

Following a bereavement there are strictly defined rules of behaviour for the family. The closest relatives observe a week of strict mourning, *shivah*, during which time they do not leave the house but sit on the floor or on low stools. In the period that follows, *shloshim*, which ends on the thirtieth day after the funeral, the conditions for observing the time of mourning are relaxed. The period of mourning for parents should last a whole year and the family should not take part in any social entertainment. When the bereaved return home from the funeral, the first meal which is laid on the table (usually prepared before their arrival by friends) consists of boiled eggs. The eggs symbolize the eternal cycle of life, birth and death.

Passover Haggadah, A prayer after a meal, Moravia, 1728

GLOSSARY

Ashkenazi	relating to the Jews who originally came from central and eastern Europe. In a wider sense the term describes the whole Ashkenazi culture.
Beracha	(pl. *Berachot*) prayers or blessings recited on various occasions. The blessing before dinner is particularly important. The prescribed answer to the word "amen".
Bimah	a platform in the centre of a synagogue at the eastern wall from which the Torah is read.
Cabbala	the Hebrew for the verb "to receive". Originally the Talmudic description of the verbal tradition, later this concept was used to describe Jewish mystical tradition. The substance of cabbala is faith in the unbroken mutual relationship between God as the eternal source of power and wisdom in the upper world and man in the world below. The main cabbalistic works are: *Sefer Yetzira* (Book of Creation), *Sefer ha-bahir* (Book of Brightness) and *Sefer ha-zohar* (Book of Splendour) attributed to Rabbi Simeon ben Jochai (2nd century). An important figure of cabbalistic teaching was Rabbi Isaac Luria, who compiled the so-called Lurian cabbala in the 16th century.
Cheder	the Hebrew for "room". The religious elementary school for children where Hebrew and the fundamental aspects of Judaism are taught. This type of school developed in the Middle Ages mainly among Ashkenazi Jews and derives its name from the classroom which was usually the front room of the teacher's house.
Diaspora	the Greek for "dispersion", Jewish settlements outside of Israel after the destruction of the first and second Temple. Later the term "diaspora" began to be used for Jewish communities overseas or abroad as opposed to Jewish settlements in the state of Israel. In a broader sense of the word, diaspora is used as an equivalent of "galut", meaning exile, captivity, expulsion.
Haggadah	the book containing the liturgy of the home service for the first two evenings of the feast of Passover.
Halacha	the portion of the Talmud that deals with laws and regulations. In the broader sense of the word, it means the entire legal system of Judaism.
Hasidism	or *Chasidism*, from the Hebrew *hasid*, meaning "affectionate", "devout". A religious and social movement whose founder was Israel ban Eliezer (1700–1760), known as Ba'al Shem Tov or "Bearer of God's name", a legendary charismatic and very influential character. Hasidism stresses the significance of ecstatic prayer, humility, joyful optimism and love for the family and community. Hasid teaching derives from the idea of the omnipresent God in the universe and the possibility of spiritual communication between the lower terrestrial and higher celestial world. Mitzvot, God's commandments, should be fulfilled with enthusiasm (*hitlahavut*), not mechanically. The belief is held that ordinary man needs a spiritual advisor or *tzaddik*.
Kiddush	traditional blessing recited over wine before the main evening meal and after the morning service on the Sabbath and festivals. If wine is not available, the blessing can be recited over two loaves of bread.
Kile	from the Hebrew *kehilah*, which means the religious community.
Kohen	or *cohen* (pl. *kohanim*), "priest" in Hebrew. The members of the tribe of Levi, the descendants of Aaron and his sons who were authorized to undertake sacred rites in the tabernacle of the covenant and in the Temple. They had special privileges but were subject to the strict laws of ritual purity. The biblical restrictions remain valid today.
Menorah	a seven-branched candelabrum, and the traditional symbol of Judaism. The original golden menorah stood in the tabernacle of the covenant in the wilderness (Ex. Chap. 25:31–40, Num. Chap. 8:2–4).
Mezuzah	a piece of parchment inscribed with scriptural passages (Deut. Chap. 6:4–9, Chap. 11:13–21), fixed to the doorpost of a Jewish house. It is placed on a decorative, metal sleeve and fixed to the right doorpost about three-quarters of the way up during a special ceremony.
Midrash	a general description for literature, originating in the Talmudic period and composed until the early Middle Ages; it interprets the significance of the biblical texts.
Mikvah	a ritual bath of purification in natural water.
Minian	or *minyan*, the Hebrew for "number". A group of men, minimum ten in number, required for religious services and ceremonies.

Mitzvah   (pl. *mitzvot*) God's commandments as described in the Torah.

Mizrach   the Hebrew for "east". It marks the direction to face when reciting prayers. In Jewish house-holds on the wall facing Jerusalem there hangs a *mizrach* picture depicting ritual motives, symbolic animals or the sign of *Magen David* ("Star of David"); various texts and a combina-tion of letters are also shown.

Omer   the Hebrew for "a sheaf of corn". A period of seven weeks extending from the second day of Passover, when the Israelites sacrificed the first sheaf called *omer*, to the first day of Shavuot when the first bread of the new harvest was sacrificed.

Sanhedrin   the Jewish council of elders and the supreme court during the period of the Jerusalem Temple.

Sephardim   Jews whose ancestors lived until their expulsion in 1492–1497 in Spain and Portugal. Now applied to Jews from the Mediterranean, Turkey and Far East.

Shammes   the synagogal servant; nowadays the man who helps to organize the service; the caretaker of the synagogue.

Shechina   God's presence in the world.

Shiviti   the plaque placed in front of the *bimah* or pedestal for the cantor on which are inscribed the introductory words of Psalm 16, 8: "I have seen the Lord always before me." It is usually dec-orated like the *mizrach*.

Sidrah   the prescribed weekly section of the Torah which is read on the Sabbath.

Talit   rectangular prayer robe worn by men during prayers.

Talmud   the Hebrew word for "learning", "studying". Also means the authoritative compilation of Jewish law and tradition. It contains the *Mishnah*, the oral law which was written down and codified about 20 CE, and the *Gemara*, which consists of supplements and commentaries to the Mishnah recorded from the 3rd to the 6th century CE. Two versions of the Talmud exist: the Palestinian or the Jerusalem, and the Babylonian.

Tefilin   small black leather boxes containing parchment of texts from the Torah attached to long leather straps. The adult Jewish man ties these around his forehead, placing the box in the centre. The straps are wrapped around left arm during the morning prayers on a week day.

Torah   the Hebrew book of teachings known as the Pentateuch (the five Books of Moses). It can be used to describe the whole of the Old Testament Bible.

Tzaddik   the Hebrew term for "righteous"; a description of an honourable, honest and devout person. According to Talmudic tradition, the world shall be redeemed thanks to the 36 righteous ones who exist in each generation. This is the name given by the Hasidim to their religious leader.

Yeshiva   the Hebrew for "session", "meeting". The school of higher Jewish education designed for the study of the Talmud.

Yiddish   the language of the Ashkenazi Jews, which was developed in the 10th–11th centuries in the Rhineland; it is a combination of German and Romanic dialects and Hebrew words and was written down phonetically using the letters of the Hebrew alphabet. Later, with the migration of the Ashkenazi Jews into central and eastern Europe, it was infiltrated with words taken from the Slavonic languages. Unlike Hebrew, the language of the educated, Yiddish was the ordinary language used for communication, the language of folklore and popular literature.

INDEX

יּוֹם וּבְכָל עֵת שֶׁחוֹנַנְתָּנוּ וְעַל אֲכִילַת מָזוֹן שָׁאַתָּה זָן וּמְפַרְנֵס אוֹתָנוּ תָּמִיד בְּכָל

צִיּוֹן מִשְׁכַּן כְּבוֹדֶךָ רַחֵם־נָא יְיָ אֱלֹהֵינוּ עַל יִשְׂרָאֵל עַמֶּךָ וְעַל יְרוּשָׁלַיִם עִירֶךָ וְ

שֶׁנִּקְרָא שִׁמְךָ כְּבוֹדֶךָ וְעַל מַלְכוּת בֵּית דָּוִד מְשִׁיחֶךָ. וְעַל הַבַּיִת הַגָּדוֹל וְהַקָּדוֹ

לָנוּ יְיָ אֱלֹהֵינוּ עָלָיו. אֱלֹהֵינוּ אָבִינוּ רְעֵנוּ זוּנֵנוּ פַּרְנְסֵנוּ וְכַלְכְּלֵנוּ וְהַרְוִיחֵנוּ וְהַרְוַ

בָּשָׂר וָדָם וְלֹא מְהֵרָה מִכָּל־צָרוֹתֵינוּ וְנָא אַל־תַּצְרִיכֵנוּ יְיָ אֱלֹהֵינוּ לֹא לִידֵי מַתְּנַת

ה שֶׁלֹּא נֵבוֹשׁ לִידֵי הַלְוָאתָם. כִּי אִם לְיָדְךָ הַמְּלֵאָה הַפְּתוּחָה הַקְּדוֹשָׁה וְהָרְחָ

הַשַּׁבָּת הַגָּדוֹל רְצֵה וְהַחֲלִיצֵנוּ יְיָ אֱלֹהֵינוּ בְּמִצְוֹתֶיךָ וּבְמִצְוַת יוֹם הַשְּׁבִיעִי.

חַ בּוֹ בְּאַהֲבָה וְהַקָּדוֹשׁ הַזֶּה. כִּי יוֹם זֶה גָּדוֹל וְקָדוֹשׁ הוּא לְפָנֶיךָ לִשְׁבָּת בּוֹ וְלָנ

וָאֲנָחָה בְּיוֹם כְּמִצְוַת רְצוֹנֶךָ: וּבִרְצוֹנְךָ הָנִיחַ לָנוּ יְיָ אֱלֹהֵינוּ שֶׁלֹּא תְהֵא צָרָה וְיָ

יר קָדְשֶׁךָ. כִּי מְנוּחָתֵנוּ. וְהַרְאֵנוּ יְיָ אֱלֹהֵינוּ בְּנֶחָמַת צִיּוֹן עִירֶךָ וּבְבִנְיַן יְרוּשָׁלַיִם

וְיִפָּקֵד וְיִזָּכֵר אֱלֹהֵינוּ וֵאלֹהֵי אֲבוֹתֵינוּ, יַעֲלֶה וְיָבֹא, וְיַגִּיעַ, וְיֵרָאֶה, וְיֵרָצֶה, וְיִשָּׁמַ

כְּרוֹן יְרוּשָׁלַיִם זִכְרוֹנֵנוּ וּפִקְדוֹנֵנוּ וְזִכְרוֹן אֲבוֹתֵינוּ. וְזִכְרוֹן מָשִׁיחַ בֶּן דָּוִד עַבְדֶּךָ: רְ

ה לְחֵן וּלְחֶסֶד עִיר קָדְשֶׁךָ. וְזִכְרוֹן כָּל עַמְּךָ בֵּית יִשְׂרָאֵל לְפָנֶיךָ. לִפְלֵטָה לְטוֹבְ

נוּ בּוֹ לְטוֹבָה וּלְרַחֲמִים לְחַיִּים וּלְשָׁלוֹם בְּיוֹם חַג הַמַּצּוֹת הַזֶּה. זָכְרֵנוּ יְיָ אֱלֹ

וְרַחֲמִים חוּס וּפָקְדֵנוּ בּוֹ לִבְרָכָה. וְהוֹשִׁיעֵנוּ בּוֹ לְחַיִּים טוֹבִים. וּבִדְבַר יְשׁוּעָ

רִיתְךָ שֶׁחָתַמְתָּ שֶׁהוֹצֵאתָנוּ יְיָ אֱלֹהֵינוּ מֵאֶרֶץ מִצְרַיִם וּפְדִיתָנוּ מִבֵּית עֲבָדִים וְעַל

יִּים חֵן וָחֶסֶד בִּבְשָׂרֵנוּ וְעַל תּוֹרָתְךָ שֶׁלִּמַּדְתָּנוּ וְעַל חֻקֶּיךָ שֶׁהוֹדַעְתָּנוּ וְעַל

יּוֹם וּבְכָל עֵת שֶׁחוֹנַנְתָּנוּ וְעַל אֲכִילַת מָזוֹן שָׁאַתָּה זָן וּמְפַרְנֵס אוֹתָנוּ תָּמִיד בְּכָ

ל צִיּוֹן מִשְׁכַּן כְּבוֹדֶךָ רַחֵם־נָא יְיָ אֱלֹהֵינוּ עַל יִשְׂרָאֵל עַמֶּךָ וְעַל יְרוּשָׁלַיִם עִירֶךָ וְ

שֶׁ שֶׁנִּקְרָא שִׁמְךָ כְּבוֹדֶךָ וְעַל מַלְכוּת בֵּית דָּוִד מְשִׁיחֶךָ. וְעַל הַבַּיִת הַגָּדוֹל וְהַקָּדוֹ

לָנוּ יְיָ אֱלֹהֵינוּ עָלָיו. אֱלֹהֵינוּ אָבִינוּ רְעֵנוּ זוּנֵנוּ פַּרְנְסֵנוּ וְכַלְכְּלֵנוּ וְהַרְוִיחֵנוּ וְהַרְוַ

בָּשָׂר וָדָם וְלֹא מְהֵרָה מִכָּל־צָרוֹתֵינוּ וְנָא אַל־תַּצְרִיכֵנוּ יְיָ אֱלֹהֵינוּ לֹא לִידֵי מַתְּנַ

ה שֶׁלֹּא נֵבוֹשׁ לִידֵי הַלְוָאתָם. כִּי אִם לְיָדְךָ הַמְּלֵאָה הַפְּתוּחָה הַקְּדוֹשָׁה וְהָרְ

הַשַּׁבָּת הַגָּדוֹל רְצֵה וְהַחֲלִיצֵנוּ יְיָ אֱלֹהֵינוּ בְּמִצְוֹתֶיךָ וּבְמִצְוַת יוֹם הַשְּׁבִיעִי.

חַ בּוֹ בְּאַהֲבָה וְהַקָּדוֹשׁ הַזֶּה. כִּי יוֹם זֶה גָּדוֹל וְקָדוֹשׁ הוּא לְפָנֶיךָ לִשְׁבָּת בּוֹ וְלָ

ן וַאֲנָחָה בְּיוֹם כְּמִצְוַת רְצוֹנֶךָ: וּבִרְצוֹנְךָ הָנִיחַ לָנוּ יְיָ אֱלֹהֵינוּ שֶׁלֹּא תְהֵא צָרָה וְ

יר קָדְשֶׁךָ. כִּי מְנוּחָתֵנוּ. וְהַרְאֵנוּ יְיָ אֱלֹהֵינוּ בְּנֶחָמַת צִיּוֹן עִירֶךָ וּבְבִנְיַן יְרוּשָׁלַיִם

צ וְיִפָּקֵד וְיִזָּכֵר אֱלֹהֵינוּ וֵאלֹהֵי אֲבוֹתֵינוּ, יַעֲלֶה וְיָבֹא, וְיַגִּיעַ, וְיֵרָאֶה, וְיֵרָצֶה, וְיִשָּׁ

כְּרוֹן יְרוּשָׁלַיִם זִכְרוֹנֵנוּ וּפִקְדוֹנֵנוּ וְזִכְרוֹן אֲבוֹתֵינוּ. וְזִכְרוֹן מָשִׁיחַ בֶּן דָּוִד עַבְדֶּךָ:

ה לְחֵן וּלְחֶסֶד עִיר קָדְשֶׁךָ. וְזִכְרוֹן כָּל עַמְּךָ בֵּית יִשְׂרָאֵל לְפָנֶיךָ. לִפְלֵטָה לְטוֹ

נוּ בּוֹ לְטוֹבָה וּלְרַחֲמִים לְחַיִּים וּלְשָׁלוֹם בְּיוֹם חַג הַמַּצּוֹת הַזֶּה. זָכְרֵנוּ יְיָ אֱל